Mastering Audio Production at Home

The Complete Guide to Creating Professional
Sound in Any Space

Shutter Sisters Studios

LateToTheParty
Publishing
BETTER LATE THAN NEVER

LateToTheParty LLC

Contents

This bookmark is for you!

Cut or tear along the vertical dotted line.

NOTES

_____

_____

_____

_____

_____

_____

_____

_____

_____

_____

_____

_____

This bookmark is for you!

Cut or tear along the vertical dotted line.

Introduction

Years ago, we found ourselves in a cramped apartment, trying to make music with a makeshift setup. Our gear was basic and our budget was tight. In that small space, we had a moment of clarity. we realized that professional-quality audio shouldn't only be for those with deep pockets or fancy studios. It should be something everyone can achieve, no matter their budget or experience level.

This book is for you. Its purpose is to empower you to achieve professional-quality audio production at home. This guide is comprehensive, practical, and budget-friendly. It breaks down the entire production process into manageable steps. You'll find it accessible whether you're a beginner or have some experience.

The world of audio production can seem complex, but our vision is to demystify it for you and provide actionable, step-by-step guidance. This book is designed to make professional-quality audio production accessible to everyone. You'll learn how to create top-notch sound without needing expensive equipment or a big studio.

What sets this book apart? First, it focuses on budget-friendly solutions. You'll find practical exercises and real-world examples tailored to different home environments and challenges. You'll learn how to get the best possible sound without breaking the bank.

Here's a brief overview of what you can expect. We'll start with setting up a home studio. You'll learn about the space, the equipment, and how to get the best sound. Next, we'll cover mastering Digital Audio Workstations (DAWs). You'll get to grips with the software that will become your main tool. Recording techniques will follow, teaching you to capture sound with clarity and precision.

We'll explore achieving the best sound quality, including developing critical listening skills and creative sound design. We'll also discuss mixing techniques in detail, showing you how to blend your tracks seamlessly. Finally, we'll discuss mastering audio, the final step in making your tracks sound polished.

Troubleshooting common issues is another key topic. You'll find solutions to problems that can arise in a home setup. Staying current with industry trends will help you keep your skills and knowledge up to date. Resourceful budgeting will show you how to make the most of what you have. You'll also find guidance on technical writing, which is essential for communicating your ideas clearly.

Each chapter includes practical exercises. These will help you apply what you've learned. You'll also find insights from industry experts, giving you a glimpse into the professional world.

We invite you to actively engage with this book's content. Try the practical exercises, participate in online communities, and use the additional resources provided. You'll find interactive tools and downloadable assets that will enhance your learning experience.

The key takeaway from this book is simple. Professional-quality audio production is achievable for everyone. No matter your budget or prior experience, you can produce top-tier audio in any home environment. This book is here to guide you every step of the way.

We have been where you are now, and we know the challenges you face. But we also know the rewards that come with overcoming those challenges. Let's embark on this journey together. Let's make great audio.

Chapter One

Fundamentals of Audio Production

We remember the first time we set up our own recording space at home. We had a microphone, an old laptop, and a lot of enthusiasm. But as soon as we hit record, something wasn't right. The audio was noisy, and the levels were all over the place. We spent hours trying to figure out what was wrong. That's when we realized the importance of understanding signal flow—how sound travels from the source to the output. This knowledge is crucial for anyone serious about audio production, and it's where we'll start our journey in this book.

1.1 Understanding Signal Flow

Signal flow is the path audio signals take from the source to the output. It's the sequence of steps that sound goes through, from the moment a microphone captures it to when it's played back through speakers or headphones. Understanding this flow is fundamental to troubleshooting and optimizing your audio quality. It helps you identify where things might be going wrong and allows you to make informed adjustments to improve your sound.

When you grasp the concept of signal flow, you'll find it easier to manage your recordings and mixes. It's like having a roadmap for your audio, guiding you through each stage of the process. Poor signal flow can lead to issues like noise, distortion, and uneven levels, which can ruin an otherwise great recording. On the other hand, a well-understood signal flow ensures that each component in your setup works harmoniously, producing clean, professional-quality audio.

To illustrate, let's break down the components of a typical signal path. It all starts with the source: your microphones and instruments. Microphones capture sound and convert it into an electrical signal. Instruments like guitars or keyboards might use pickups or direct input (DI) boxes to do the same. This initial signal is crucial because any issues here will carry through the entire signal path.

Next, the signal passes through preamps and interfaces. Preamps amplify the weak signals from microphones to a level suitable for recording. Audio interfaces convert these analog signals into digital data that your computer and Digital Audio Workstation (DAW) can process. The quality of your preamps and interface can significantly impact your sound, so choose wisely.

Once in the DAW, the signal can be manipulated in countless ways. This is where you'll mix, edit, and apply effects. Mixing consoles or virtual mixers in your DAW allows you to balance levels, pan tracks, and route signals to different effects processors. Effects processors, whether hardware or software plugins, add reverb, delay, compression, and other effects to shape your sound.

Finally, the processed signal is sent back through the audio interface to your monitors or headphones for playback. Monitors are specialized speakers designed for accurate audio reproduction, which is essential for making informed mixing decisions. Headphones are also valuable for detailed listening, especially when you need to hear subtle nuances in your mix.

Common signal flow issues can disrupt this process, but understanding the flow helps you troubleshoot efficiently. Poor connections or low-quality cables often cause signal degradation and noise. Make sure all your cables are intact, and use high-quality connectors. Latency and phase issues can arise from improper synchronization between devices. Adjust your DAW settings to minimize latency, and use phase alignment tools if necessary.

Routing errors and feedback loops are other common problems. These occur when signals are incorrectly routed or fed back into themselves, causing unwanted noise and distortion. Always double-check your routing settings and ensure your signal paths are clear and logical.

To put theory into practice, start with a simple exercise. Set up a basic recording chain: connect a microphone to your preamp, route it through your audio interface, and record into your DAW. Create a signal flow chart to visualize each step, from the microphone to the monitors. This exercise will help you understand each component's role and how they interact.

Next, troubleshoot a mock signal flow issue. For instance, simulate a scenario where you hear unwanted noise in your recording. Trace the signal path from the source to the output, identifying potential problem areas. Check your connections, settings, and equipment to find and resolve the issue.

Mastering signal flow is your first step toward professional audio production. It's the foundation upon which all other skills are built. Once you understand how sound travels through your setup, you'll be better equipped to tackle more advanced topics like mixing, mastering, and creative sound design. Let's get started on this exciting journey together.

1.2 Basics of Acoustics for Home Studios

Acoustics play a crucial role in how sound behaves within any given space. Understanding these principles is vital for achieving high-quality audio production at home. Sound waves are essentially vibrations that travel through the air and interact with the room they're in. These interactions can significantly affect the clarity and quality of your recordings. Sound waves have properties like wavelength, frequency, and amplitude, which influence how they are perceived. When sound waves encounter surfaces, they can reflect, absorb, or diffuse. Reflection occurs when sound bounces off a surface, often causing echo and reverb. Absorption happens when a surface, like acoustic foam, soaks up the sound energy, reducing reflections. Diffusion scatters sound waves in different directions, helping to create a more even sound field. Understanding these behaviors is key to managing your recording environment effectively.

One of the most significant challenges in home studios is dealing with room modes and standing waves. Room modes are specific frequencies that resonate more intensely due to the room's dimensions. These can create peaks and nulls in the frequency response, making some frequencies overly loud and others almost inaudible. Standing waves occur when sound waves reflect between two parallel surfaces, like walls, creating constructive and destructive interference areas. These phenomena can severely impact the accuracy of your monitoring environment, making it challenging to produce balanced mixes.

Small room acoustics pose another set of challenges. The limited space often leads to more pronounced reflections and standing waves. Background noise from household activities or external sources like traffic can also interfere with recordings. These noises can introduce unwanted artifacts and reduce the clarity of your audio. Addressing these issues is crucial for creating a controlled and professional-sounding environment.

Improving home studio acoustics doesn't have to be expensive. One effective solution is to build your own acoustic panels and bass traps. These can be constructed using materials like mineral wool or fiberglass insulation covered with fabric. Placing these panels at first reflection points—areas where sound first hits a wall—can significantly reduce reflections. Bass traps, which are thicker and denser, should be placed in corners to absorb low-frequency energy. This helps to manage room modes and create a more balanced frequency response.

Strategic placement of acoustic treatments can make a world of difference. Start by positioning your speakers along the shorter wall of a rectangular room, with the listening position set up at an equilateral triangle from the speakers. This minimizes reflections from sidewalls. Place acoustic panels at the first reflection points on the side walls and ceiling to absorb early reflections. Bass traps should be positioned in the corners, where low-frequency buildup is most problematic. If you're on a tight budget, even household items like bookshelves, rugs, and heavy curtains can help control reflections and improve the sound quality.

Let's look at a real-world example. A friend of ours transformed his small bedroom into a recording space with a few simple steps. He identified the first reflection points and placed DIY acoustic panels made from mineral wool and fabric. Next, he built bass traps for the corners using dense insulation. He added a thick rug on the floor and heavy curtains over the windows to further improve the acoustics. The result was a dramatically reduced reflection and a much clearer, more accurate sound. This setup allowed him to produce professional-quality recordings without spending a fortune.

Different room sizes and shapes require tailored solutions. In a large room, you might need more extensive acoustic treatment to manage reflections and standing waves. In a small, irregularly shaped room, strategically placed panels and traps can help control the sound. For example, in an L-shaped room, placing bass traps in the corners of the primary recording area and panels along the walls can create a controlled environment. The key is to experiment with placement and materials to find what works best for your specific space.

Understanding and implementing these acoustic principles can transform your home studio. By addressing the challenges and applying practical, budget-friendly solutions, you can create an environment that allows your recordings to shine. This foundation will serve you well as you continue to develop your skills and produce high-quality audio in any space.

1.3 Essential Audio Production Terminology

Understanding key terms and concepts is crucial in the world of audio production. These terms are the building blocks of your work, enabling you to communicate effectively and make informed decisions. Let's start with some of the most fundamental terms: gain, EQ, compression, and reverb.

Gain refers to the amount of amplification applied to an audio signal. It determines how loud the signal is before it enters the recording or mixing chain. Proper gain staging is essential to avoid distortion and maintain audio clarity. For example, when recording vocals, setting the gain too high can cause clipping, resulting in unpleasant distortion. Conversely, setting it too low will make the recording too quiet, requiring excessive amplification later, which can introduce noise. Always aim for a balanced gain setting that allows you to capture the full dynamic range of the performance without distortion.

EQ, or equalization, is the process of adjusting the balance between different frequency components in an audio signal. It allows you to shape the sound by boosting or cutting specific frequencies. In a mix, EQ is used to carve out space for each instrument, ensuring they don't mask each other. For example, if a vocal track competes with a guitar in the same frequency range, you can use EQ to reduce the guitar's presence in that range, allowing the vocal to shine through. This technique, known as subtractive EQ, is invaluable for creating a clear and balanced mix.

Compression is a dynamic range control tool that reduces the difference between the loudest and quietest parts of an audio signal. By taming peaks and raising the level of quieter sections, compression helps achieve a more consistent and polished sound. For instance, applying compression to a drum track can make the kick and snare hit more even, giving the rhythm section a tighter and more controlled feel. However, over-compression can squash the dynamics, making the track sound lifeless, so use it judiciously.

Reverb, short for reverberation, simulates the way sound reflects and decays in a physical space. It adds depth and ambiance to recordings, making them sound more natural and immersive. For example, adding reverb to a dry vocal recording can make it sound as if it was performed in a concert hall, adding a sense of space and grandeur. Different types of reverb, such as plate, hall, and room, offer various sonic characteristics, allowing you to choose the best one for your mix.

Another important concept is the Signal-to-Noise Ratio (SNR). SNR measures the level of the desired signal compared to the level of background noise. A higher SNR indicates a cleaner, clearer recording with less noise. Maintaining a high SNR is crucial for professional-quality audio. This involves using good-quality equipment, proper gain staging, and minimizing noise sources.

Digital audio basics like bit depth and sample rate are also fundamental. Bit depth determines the dynamic range of the audio signal, with higher bit depths allowing for more detail and nuance. For example, 24-bit audio provides a greater dynamic range than 16-bit audio, capturing more subtle details in the recording. Sample rate refers to the number of samples taken per second to represent the audio signal digitally. Higher sample rates capture more detail, with 44.1 kHz being standard for CDs and 48 kHz for video production. Choosing the right sample rate depends on your project's requirements and the desired audio quality.

Practical application of these terms solidifies understanding. Adjusting gain for a vocal recording involves setting the input level so the loudest parts of the performance don't clip while ensuring the quiet parts are captured clearly. Using EQ to carve out space in a mix might involve reducing the low-mid frequencies of a guitar track to make room for the bass guitar, ensuring each instrument occupies its own sonic space. Choosing the right sample rate for a project ensures you capture the necessary detail without using excessive storage or processing power.

For quick reference, here's a glossary of essential audio production terms:

- Gain: Amplification level of an audio signal.

- EQ (Equalization): Adjusting the balance of frequency components.

- Compression: Controlling the dynamic range of an audio signal.

- Reverb: Simulating reflections and decay in a physical space.

- SNR (Signal-to-Noise Ratio): Ratio of desired signal level to background noise level.

- Bit Depth: Determines the dynamic range of digital audio.

- Sample Rate: Number of samples per second in digital audio.

Understanding and applying these terms will greatly enhance your audio production skills. These concepts are the foundation upon which professional-quality recordings and mixes are built. By mastering these basics, you'll be well-equipped to tackle more advanced topics and produce exceptional audio in any setting.

Chapter Two

Setting Up Your Home Studio

We remember the first time we stepped into a professional recording studio. The pristine acoustics, top-tier equipment, and meticulously arranged setup were awe-inspiring. It was a far cry from the cluttered corner of our bedroom where we had our DIY studio. But that experience sparked a realization: you don't need a high-end studio to create professional-quality sound. With the right approach, you can transform any space into a functional home studio.

2.1 Choosing the Right Space for Audio Production

Selecting the perfect room for your home studio can be a game-changer. The size and shape of the room play pivotal roles in determining the quality of your recordings. Ideally, you want a rectangular room, as it helps to manage acoustic reflections more effectively than square or irregularly shaped spaces. A room that's too large can cause excessive reverb, while a space that's too small might amplify unwanted reflections and standing waves. The balance lies in finding a medium-sized room where you can control the sound without feeling too cramped or too echoey.

Soundproofing potential is another critical factor. A room with thick walls and minimal windows will naturally keep external noise at bay. However, not everyone has access to such spaces. If you're working in a room with thin walls or near a busy street, you'll need to consider additional soundproofing methods. This could involve adding mass to the walls, using soundproof curtains, or even creating a room within a room to isolate the sound. The goal is to create a controlled environment where external noise doesn't interfere with your recordings.

Ambient noise levels can make or break your recordings. Choose a room away from household noise, like the kitchen or living room. Basements and attics often work well because they're generally more isolated from the hustle and bustle of daily life. However, they come with their own challenges, such as temperature control and ventilation, which must be addressed to ensure a comfortable recording environment.

Accessibility and convenience should not be overlooked. Your studio should be easy to access, especially if you plan on spending long hours working on your projects. It's a bonus if the room has enough space to store your gear and allows for a comfortable workflow. A cluttered or inconvenient space can hinder your creativity and productivity.

When evaluating different types of spaces, bedrooms, and spare rooms are often the first choices for many home studio enthusiasts. They're usually easier to soundproof and are conveniently located within the house. However, they might require some adjustments, like moving furniture or adding acoustic treatments. Basements and attics offer more isolation but might need significant soundproofing and climate control. Garages and sheds can be excellent alternatives if properly insulated and soundproofed, providing a spacious area to set up your studio.

In less-than-ideal spaces, you can use rugs and curtains to reduce reflections and improve acoustics. Rugs can help absorb sound on the floor, while heavy curtains can dampen reflections from windows and walls. Arranging furniture strategically can also make a significant difference. Bookshelves filled with books act as natural diffusers, breaking up sound waves and reducing reflections. Placing a sofa or chairs can help absorb some sound and improve the room's acoustics.

Basic soundproofing techniques can also enhance your studio's environment. Sealing gaps in doors and windows with weather stripping can reduce noise leakage. Adding acoustic panels to walls and ceilings can help control reflections and improve sound quality. These panels can be DIY projects or purchased from specialized suppliers. The key is to address the most reflective surfaces to create a balanced and controlled acoustic environment.

Real-World Examples and Layouts

Take the example of a friend who converted his living room corner into a recording space. He used a thick rug to cover the hardwood floor and hung heavy curtains around the recording area to dampen reflections. Bookshelves filled with books acted as diffusers, and he strategically placed a few acoustic panels on the walls. The result was a cozy, functional studio that produced surprisingly professional recordings.

Another example is a small attic conversion. The owner used thick insulation to manage temperature and soundproofing. Acoustic panels were placed on the sloped ceiling to control reflections, and a bass trap was added in the corner to manage low frequencies. The setup included a small desk for the computer and audio interface, with speakers positioned at ear level. Despite the attic's size constraints, the space felt open and clear, perfect for focused audio work.

These examples show that with some creativity and the right strategies, you can optimize any space for audio production. The key is to understand the room's challenges and address them with practical solutions. Whether you're working with a spacious basement or a tiny bedroom corner, the principles of good acoustic treatment and smart arrangement apply universally.

2.2 Budget-Friendly Acoustic Treatments

When we first started working on our home studio, we quickly realized that the room's acoustics were affecting our recordings. Unwanted reflections made the sound muddy, and the bass frequencies were all over the place. Proper acoustic treatment can drastically improve your recording and mixing quality. By reducing unwanted reflections, you can achieve a cleaner sound. Controlling bass frequencies helps prevent them from overwhelming the mix, enhancing clarity and accuracy. This way, what you hear while mixing closely matches what listeners will hear on their devices.

Building your own acoustic panels is a cost-effective method to treat your home studio. You can make these panels using materials like mineral wool or fiberglass insulation, wooden frames, and breathable fabric. The process is straightforward: construct a wooden frame, fill it with insulation, and cover it with fabric. These panels absorb sound waves, reducing reflections and improving the overall sound quality of your room. Creating bass traps with household materials is another budget-friendly option. Use thick insulation or even tightly packed towels rolled inside fabric. Place these traps in the corners of your room where bass frequencies tend to build up.

Temporary treatments like blankets and pillows can also help. While not as effective as dedicated acoustic panels, they can still make a noticeable difference. Hang heavy blankets on walls and over windows to dampen reflections. Place pillows in corners to help absorb bass frequencies. These temporary solutions are particularly useful if you're on a tight budget or need a quick fix before investing in more permanent treatments.

Proper placement of acoustic treatments is crucial for maximum effectiveness. Start with the first reflection points. These are the spots where sound waves first bounce off walls, ceiling, and floor before reaching your ears. Use a mirror to identify these points: have someone move a mirror along the walls while you sit in your usual listening position. Wherever you see the speaker's reflection in the mirror, place an acoustic panel there. This reduces early reflections and helps create a clearer sound.

Bass traps should be placed in the corners of the room, both vertically and horizontally. Bass frequencies tend to accumulate in corners, causing muddiness and resonance issues. Placing bass traps in these areas helps absorb these low frequencies, resulting in a tighter and more controlled bass response. Don't forget about the ceiling and floor. While it's challenging to treat the floor without carpeting, adding a thick rug can help. For the ceiling, consider placing panels above your listening position to further reduce reflections.

Case Study: Transforming a Small Room with Minimal Investment

Let's take a look at a real-world example. Sarah, a budding music producer, had a small, square room she wanted to convert into a home studio. The room had bare walls and a hardwood floor, making it highly reflective. Sarah started by building her own acoustic panels using mineral wool, wooden frames, and fabric. She placed these panels at the first reflection points on the walls and ceiling. Next, she created bass traps using thick insulation wrapped in fabric and positioned them in the room's corners.

To further improve the acoustics, Sarah hung heavy curtains over the windows and added a thick rug on the floor. She even used some pillows in the remaining corners to help with low-frequency absorption. The transformation was remarkable. The room went from a highly reflective, echoey space to a controlled environment with clear sound. Sarah's recordings and mixes improved significantly, all without breaking the bank.

Photos of DIY acoustic treatments can provide inspiration and guidance. Before-and-after images of treated rooms show a drastic improvement in sound quality. Seeing how others have successfully transformed their spaces can motivate you to start your acoustic treatment project. Remember, the goal is to create a balanced and controlled environment that enhances your recording and mixing efforts.

By implementing these budget-friendly acoustic treatments, you can drastically improve your home studio's sound quality. Whether you build your own panels, use temporary solutions like blankets and pillows, or strategically place bass traps, each step brings you closer to achieving professional-quality audio in your home studio.

2.3 Essential Gear and Setup for Beginners

Starting your home studio journey can feel overwhelming with the plethora of gear available on the market. However, focusing on the essentials can simplify the process and set you up for success. The cornerstone of any home studio is a reliable audio interface. This device connects your microphone and instruments to your computer, converting analog signals into digital data that your DAW (Digital Audio Workstation) can process. Look for an interface with multiple inputs and outputs to accommodate various recording needs. The Focusrite Scarlett 2i2 is a fantastic budget-friendly option that offers excellent preamps and ease of use.

Microphones are another critical component. For vocals and acoustic instruments, condenser microphones are generally preferred due to their sensitivity and clarity. The Audio-Technica AT2020 is a solid, affordable choice that delivers impressive performance. On the other hand, dynamic microphones like the Shure SM57 are robust and versatile, making them ideal for recording louder sound sources like guitar amps and drums.

Monitoring your recordings accurately is crucial, so invest in good-quality headphones and studio monitors. Headphones allow you to hear the finer details of your recordings without external noise interference. The Audio-Technica M50x offers excellent sound quality at a reasonable price. Studio monitors, like the JBL 305P MkII, provide a flat frequency response, ensuring that what you hear is a true representation of your mix. This accuracy is vital for making informed mixing decisions.

Your DAW is the software hub where all your recording, editing, and mixing take place. Beginners often start with free or affordable options like GarageBand or Reaper, which offer robust features without breaking the bank. As you progress, you might consider upgrading to more advanced software like Logic Pro X or Ableton Live, both of which are industry standards known for their versatility and powerful features.

Cables and stands often get overlooked but are fundamental to a smooth workflow. XLR cables connect your microphones to the audio interface, while TRS cables are used for connecting monitors. Invest in durable, high-quality cables to avoid connectivity issues. Microphone stands are essential for positioning your mics correctly, ensuring stable and consistent recordings. Adjustable stands with boom arms, like the K&M stands, provide flexibility and ease of use.

When selecting gear, focus on features that offer the best value for your budget. For audio interfaces, prioritize those with high-quality preamps and low latency. Multiple inputs and outputs are beneficial if you plan on recording multiple sources simultaneously. For microphones, consider whether you need a condenser or dynamic mic based on your primary recording needs. Condenser mics are great for capturing detailed vocals and acoustic instruments, while dynamic mics are more rugged and versatile.

Studio monitors should have a flat frequency response to ensure accurate monitoring. Avoid monitors that excessively color the sound, as this can lead to misleading mix decisions. Entry-level monitors like the KRK Rokit 5 G4 offer a good balance between price and performance, making them ideal for beginners. When it comes to DAWs, choose one that aligns with your workflow and offers the features you need. GarageBand is excellent for beginners due to its user-friendly interface, while Reaper provides extensive customization options for those who want more control.

Setting up your gear correctly is crucial for optimal performance. Start by connecting your audio interface to your computer via USB or Thunderbolt. Install any necessary drivers and configure the interface settings in your DAW. Next, connect your microphone to the audio interface using an XLR cable. Place the microphone on a stand and position it according to the sound source. For vocals, the mic should be at mouth level, about 6-12 inches away, with a pop filter to reduce plosives.

Monitoring through headphones and studio monitors requires proper setup to avoid latency and ensure accurate playback. Connect your headphones to the audio interface's headphone output and your monitors to the main outputs. Adjust the interface's monitoring settings to balance between direct monitoring and DAW playback. If you encounter latency issues, lower the buffer size in your DAW settings, but be mindful that this might increase CPU usage.

Troubleshooting common issues can save you a lot of headaches. If your computer doesn't recognize your audio interface, ensure the drivers are installed correctly and check the connections. For latency problems, adjusting the buffer size usually helps. If you experience connectivity issues with your cables, inspect them for any damage or loose connections. Replacing faulty cables can often resolve these problems.

With the right gear and setup, you're well on your way to creating professional-quality audio at home. The next step is mastering the tools and techniques to elevate your recordings and mixes to the next level.

Chapter Three

Mastering Your Digital Audio Workstation (DAW)

The first time we opened Pro Tools, we were overwhelmed by the sheer number of options and controls. We remember feeling both excited and intimidated, not knowing where to begin. But as we spent more time with it, we began to appreciate its power and versatility. It became clear that mastering this tool would be key to achieving professional-quality audio. This chapter aims to guide you through the essentials of Pro Tools, making it accessible whether you're just starting out or looking to refine your skills.

3.1 Pro Tools: A Step-by-Step Guide

Pro Tools is revered for its robust capabilities and is a staple in many professional studios. Its interface, while complex at first glance, is designed for efficiency and precision. The main windows you'll work with are the Edit and Mix windows. The Edit window is your primary workspace, where you can view and manipulate your audio tracks in a timeline format. This is where you'll spend most of your time editing and arranging your audio. The Mix window, on the other hand, resembles a traditional mixing console. Here, you can adjust levels, panning, and insert effects.

Navigating these windows is made easier with the toolbar, which contains essential functions and shortcuts. The toolbar includes tools like the Selector, Grabber, and Trimmer, each serving a specific purpose in editing audio. For instance, the Selector tool allows you to highlight sections of audio for editing, while the Grabber tool lets you move clips around. Shortcuts, such as pressing 'R' and 'T' to zoom in and out, can significantly speed up your workflow once you get the hang of them.

Customizing your workspace in Pro Tools is another way to enhance your efficiency. You can arrange the windows and toolbars to suit your preferences, making frequently used tools more accessible. Saving your workspace layout ensures you can quickly return to your preferred setup, even after closing and reopening the software.

Starting a new session in Pro Tools is straightforward but critical for setting the foundation of your project. Begin by opening Pro Tools and selecting "Create New Session." You'll then be prompted to name your session and choose a location to save it. Next, set the sample rate and bit depth. These settings determine the audio quality of your recordings. For most projects, a sample rate of 44.1 kHz and a bit depth of 24 bits are standard. However, if you're working on a high-fidelity project, you might opt for higher settings.

Once your session is created, you can import audio files. This can be done by selecting "Import Audio" from the File menu. Choose the files you want to import, and Pro Tools will place them into your session. This is useful for bringing in pre-recorded tracks or samples you'll be working with.

Recording and editing audio in Pro Tools is where the software truly shines. To start recording, you'll need to arm the tracks you want to record on by clicking the record enable button on each track. This primes them to receive audio input. Use the transport controls—play, stop, record, etc.—to manage your recording session. When you're ready, hit the record button on the transport bar and start capturing your audio.

Editing tools like Trim, Fade, and Crossfade are your best friends in the editing process. The Trim tool allows you to shorten or extend audio clips, helping you clean up unwanted noise or silence. Fades help to smooth out the beginning and end of audio clips, eliminating abrupt starts and stops. Crossfades are particularly useful for seamlessly blending two audio clips together, making transitions sound natural.

Mixing in Pro Tools involves balancing the levels of different tracks to create a cohesive sound. The Mix window is where you'll do most of this work. Here, you can insert plugins to add effects like EQ, compression, and reverb. Adjusting parameters within these plugins allows you to shape the sound of each track to fit your overall mix. For instance, using an EQ plugin to carve out frequencies can help different instruments sit better together in the mix.

Automation is another powerful feature in Pro Tools. It allows you to automate changes in volume, panning, and effects over time. This is useful for creating dynamic mixes that evolve throughout the track. To automate a parameter, simply enable automation for that parameter and draw in the changes using the pencil tool.

Quick Reference Checklist

- Create New Session: Name your session and set the sample rate and bit depth.

- Import Audio Files: Bring in any pre-recorded tracks or samples.

- Arm Tracks for Recording: Click the record enable button on each track.

- Use Transport Controls: Manage your recording with play, stop, and record buttons.

- Trim and Fade Tools: Clean up and smooth out your audio clips.

- Mix Window: Balance levels and insert plugins for effects.

- Automation: Enable and draw in changes for dynamic mixes.

Pro Tools is powerful, but its mastery of features truly sets your work apart. You can achieve professional-quality audio from your home studio by understanding the interface, setting up sessions correctly, and utilizing the various recording, editing, and mixing tools.

3.2 Navigating Ableton Live Efficiently

Ableton Live stands out with its intuitive, minimalist interface designed to streamline music creation and live performance. The software features two main views: Session and Arrangement. Session View is ideal for improvisation and live performances, offering a grid layout where you can launch audio or MIDI clips in real-time. This view fosters creativity, allowing you to experiment with different loops and ideas without disrupting the flow. Arrangement View, on the other hand, is more linear and traditional, much like a multitrack tape recorder. Here, you can arrange your clips into a complete song, making it perfect for detailed editing and finalizing your projects.

Navigating Ableton Live is straightforward, thanks to its user-friendly design. The interface is customizable, letting you arrange windows and toolbars to suit your workflow. The main navigation bar at the top provides quick access to essential tools and functions. You can split the screen to view both Session and Arrangement views simultaneously, offering flexibility in how you manage your projects. The Browser on the left side is your go-to for managing files and plugins. It's divided into categories like Instruments, Audio Effects, and Samples, making it easy to find what you need. You can drag and drop items directly from the Browser into your project, streamlining the workflow.

Creating and managing tracks in Ableton Live is a breeze. You can create two main types of tracks: Audio and MIDI. Audio tracks are for recording vocals and instruments or importing audio files. MIDI tracks, on the other hand, are for virtual instruments and sequencing MIDI notes. To create a new track, simply right-click in the track area and choose the type you need. Return tracks are used to send audio signals to effects, like reverb or delay, and can be shared by multiple tracks. Grouping tracks is another powerful feature, allowing you to organize and process multiple tracks as a single unit. This is particularly useful for managing complex projects with many layers. Track templates can save you time by allowing you to create and save a set of tracks with predefined settings, which you can load into any project.

Recording and sequencing MIDI in Ableton Live opens up a world of possibilities. Start by setting up your MIDI instruments, either by connecting a MIDI keyboard or using virtual instruments within the software. Recording MIDI clips is as simple as hitting the record button and playing your instrument. Once recorded, you can edit MIDI notes and velocities in the Piano Roll, where you can see each note's pitch and duration. The Drum Rack is a specialized device for sequencing drum patterns, providing an intuitive grid layout for drum programming. You can drag and drop samples into the Drum Rack pads, making it easy to create custom drum kits.

Ableton Live's unique features set it apart from other DAWs. Warping and time-stretching audio are standout capabilities. Warping allows you to manipulate the timing of audio clips without affecting their pitch, making it easy to sync samples and loops to your project's tempo. This feature is invaluable for remixing and live DJ sets, where matching beats is crucial. The Session View, designed for live performance, lets you trigger clips and scenes on the fly, offering unparalleled flexibility for live shows. Max for

Live is another game-changer that integrates Max/MSP programming into Ableton Live. This allows you to create custom devices, from unique audio effects to complex MIDI controllers, expanding the software's capabilities exponentially.

Navigating Ableton Live efficiently means leveraging these features to enhance your workflow. Use the Browser to quickly access and organize your files and plugins. Customize your workspace to keep essential tools within reach. Create track templates to streamline your setup process. Record and sequence MIDI with precision using the Piano Roll and Drum Rack. Experiment with warping and time-stretching to sync your audio clips seamlessly. Utilize Max for Live to push the boundaries of your creativity. By mastering these aspects of Ableton Live, you can transform your home studio into a powerhouse of music production and live performance.

3.3 Getting Started with Logic Pro

Logic Pro is a powerhouse DAW that combines user-friendly features with professional-grade capabilities. When you first open Logic Pro, you'll notice its clean and intuitive interface. The main windows you'll interact with are the Tracks area, the Mixer, and the Library. The Tracks area is where you'll arrange your audio and MIDI tracks. It's similar to a traditional multitrack tape recorder, allowing you to see everything in a timeline. The Mixer window gives you a visual representation of your mix, complete with faders, pan knobs, and plugin slots. The Library is where you'll find all your instruments, loops, and presets, making it easy to drag and drop elements into your project.

Navigating Logic Pro becomes second nature once you familiarize yourself with its toolbars and key commands. The toolbar at the top of the screen offers quick access to essential functions like recording, editing, and mixing. You can customize this toolbar to include the tools you use most frequently, streamlining your workflow. Key commands are shortcuts that allow you to perform actions quickly. For instance, pressing 'X' opens the Mixer window, while 'P' opens the Piano Roll editor. Learning these shortcuts can save you a lot of time.

Customizing the interface layout is another way to make Logic Pro work for you. You can rearrange windows, resize panels, and even save your custom layouts. This flexibility allows you to create a workspace that suits your needs, whether you're focusing on recording, editing, or mixing. For example, you might have one layout for tracking with the Tracks area and Mixer prominent and another for mixing with the Mixer and Plugin windows front and center.

Setting up a new project in Logic Pro is straightforward but crucial for a smooth workflow. Start by opening Logic Pro and selecting "New Project." You'll be prompted to choose a template or start with an empty project. After selecting your preference, you'll set the project parameters like tempo, key, and time signature. These settings can be adjusted later, but it's good to have a starting point. Importing and organizing audio files is simple: drag your files into the Tracks area or use the Import Audio function. Logic Pro automatically organizes these files into tracks, making it easy to start working on your project.

Recording and editing both audio and MIDI tracks is where Logic Pro excels. To set up an audio track, click the '+' button above the Tracks area and select 'Audio.' For MIDI tracks, select 'Software Instrument.' This will open a new track with a default instrument loaded. Recording is as easy as hitting the record button in the transport bar. For audio, make sure your inputs are set correctly, and your levels are adjusted to avoid clipping. For MIDI, ensure your MIDI controller is connected and recognized by Logic Pro. Once you've recorded your tracks, you can use the Editor for precision editing. The Editor allows you to trim, cut, and move audio clips with ease. Flex Time and Flex Pitch are powerful tools in Logic Pro that let you manipulate the timing and pitch of your recordings without degrading the audio quality. Flex Time is perfect for tightening up performances, while Flex Pitch is great for correcting or enhancing vocal intonation.

Mixing in Logic Pro is a comprehensive experience thanks to its built-in plugins and effects. The Mixer window is your main hub for balancing levels, panning tracks, and applying effects. Logic Pro comes with a suite of high-quality plugins, including EQ, compression, and reverb. These tools allow you to shape your sound precisely. Applying and adjusting plugins is as simple as selecting a slot on a track and choosing the desired effect. You can then tweak the parameters to fit your mix. For example, using the Channel EQ plugin, you can carve out frequencies to give each instrument its own space in the mix. Compression helps control dynamics, making sure no part of the track is too loud or too quiet. Reverb adds depth and space, making your recordings sound more natural and polished.

Automation in Logic Pro is another powerful feature that lets you create dynamic mixes. You can automate volume, panning, and plugin parameters to change over time. This is useful for adding movement and interest to your tracks. For instance, you might automate a gradual increase in reverb during a chorus to make it sound bigger. To enable automation, click the 'A' button on the toolbar, then draw in your automation curves directly on the tracks.

Logic Pro's unique instruments and effects set it apart from other DAWs. From the Alchemy synth, which offers a vast array of sounds and modulation options, to the Space Designer reverb, which allows for creating custom reverb spaces, Logic Pro's tools are top-notch. These instruments and effects are powerful and user-friendly, making them accessible to both beginners and advanced users.

Interactive Element: Practical Exercise

- Create a New Project: Open Logic Pro and start a new project. Set the tempo, key, and time signature.

- Set Up Tracks: Add both audio and MIDI tracks. Record a short vocal line and a MIDI drum pattern.

- Use Flex Tools: Apply Flex Time to tighten the vocal performance and Flex Pitch to adjust any off-key notes.

- Mixing: Use the Mixer window to balance the levels. Apply EQ to the vocal track, compression to the drum track, and reverb to both.

- Automation: Automate a volume fade-out at the end of your project.

With Logic Pro, you're equipped to create, record, and mix your music with professional quality. Understanding its interface, setting up projects efficiently, and leveraging its powerful tools will elevate your audio production capabilities.

Chapter Four

Recording Techniques

The first time we recorded vocals at home, we were excited but quickly frustrated. The recordings sounded flat, full of unwanted echoes and strange resonances. We soon realized the importance of room acoustics in capturing high-quality vocals. Your room can significantly affect the clarity and warmth of your recordings. Uncontrolled reflections can muddy the sound, making your vocals less defined. This is why considering your recording environment is crucial.

4.1 Capturing Vocals at Home

Room acoustics play a pivotal role in vocal recording. When sound waves hit hard surfaces, they reflect back, causing echoes and reverberations that can muddy your recordings. To combat this, you might consider using portable vocal booths. These compact, cost-effective solutions can drastically improve your vocal clarity without the need for extensive room treatment. For instance, artists like Ariana Grande and Ty Dolla $ign have utilized portable recording booths to capture clean vocals at home. These booths, such as the Snap Studio Ultimate Vocal Booth or the SE Electronics Reflexion Filter PRO, are designed to absorb sound, reduce reflections, and isolate vocal performance.

Positioning the singer in the room also matters. Ideally, avoid placing the singer in the center of the room where reflections are most pronounced. Instead, position them about a third of the way into the room, away from walls and hard surfaces. This placement helps minimize unwanted reflections. Additionally, using reflection filters behind the microphone can further absorb sound, preventing it from bouncing back into the mic.

Microphone selection and placement are crucial for capturing the best vocal performance. Condenser microphones are generally preferred for their sensitivity and clarity. They capture a wide range of frequencies, making vocals sound more detailed. Dynamic microphones, such as the Shure SM7B, are excellent for handling louder sounds and reducing background noise. The choice depends on the vocalist's style and the recording environment.

The distance from the microphone is another important factor. Typically, placing the singer about six to twelve inches away from the mic works well. This distance captures the nuances of the voice without introducing too much proximity effect, which can make the vocals sound boomy. Adjust the angle and height of the microphone to suit the singer's position. A slight tilt can reduce plosives—those harsh "p" and "b" sounds—and capture a more natural tone.

Vocal recording techniques can make a significant difference in the final sound. Proper gain staging ensures you capture a strong signal without clipping. Aim for vocal levels between -12 and -18 dB to maintain headroom and avoid distortion. Using a pop filter in front of the microphone can reduce plosives and sibilance, making the recording smoother. Pop filters are simple mesh screens that diffuse the air from plosive sounds before they hit the microphone diaphragm.

Coaching and directing the vocalist during the session can also improve the recording. Encourage the singer to perform multiple takes to capture the best possible performance. Provide clear feedback and support, helping them relax and deliver their best. A comfortable and confident vocalist will produce a better recording.

Troubleshooting common vocal recording issues can save you time and frustration. Sibilance, or harsh "s" sounds, can be managed by adjusting the microphone angle or using a de-esser plugin during mixing. Controlling breath noise involves coaching the singer on breathing techniques and using a pop filter. Room reflections and ambient noise can be minimized with portable vocal booths and reflection filters.

Managing sibilance and harsh frequencies is often a matter of mic placement and post-production techniques. Adjusting the mic angle slightly off-axis can reduce sibilance. Using a de-esser plugin during mixing can also help control these harsh sounds. Controlling breath noise involves coaching the singer to manage their breathing and using a pop filter to diffuse the air.

Dealing with room reflections and ambient noise is crucial for a clean recording. Portable vocal booths and reflection filters can significantly reduce these issues. Additionally, recording during quieter times of the day and using heavy curtains or blankets to cover reflective surfaces can help. Ensuring a quiet and controlled environment will result in clearer, more professional vocal recordings.

By paying attention to room acoustics, selecting the right microphone, and employing proper recording techniques, you can capture high-quality vocals at home. Remember, the goal is to create a controlled environment that allows the vocalist's performance to shine.

4.2 Recording Acoustic Instruments in a Small Space

Recording acoustic instruments in a small space presents unique challenges that can affect the quality of your recordings. One of the primary issues is limited space for mic placement. In a cramped environment, finding the optimal position for your microphones can be difficult. You need enough room to experiment with different positions to capture the best sound, but small spaces often don't allow for this flexibility. Additionally, excessive room reflections can muddy your recordings. Hard surfaces like walls and ceilings reflect sound waves, creating unwanted echoes and reverb. This can make your recordings sound less clear and more cluttered. Ambient noise and interference from outside the room can also be problematic. Whether it's traffic noise, household sounds, or even the hum of electrical appliances, these unwanted noises can easily find their way into your recordings.

Choosing the right microphone and placing it correctly can mitigate many of these issues. For recording acoustic instruments, both small diaphragm and large diaphragm condenser mics have their uses. Small diaphragm condensers are great for capturing detailed, high-frequency content, making them ideal for instruments like acoustic guitar and violin. On the other hand, large diaphragm condensers excel in capturing the warmth and body of an instrument, which is useful for recording instruments like the piano. Stereo mic techniques like XY, ORTF, and spaced pair can also enhance your recordings. The XY technique, where two mics are placed at a 90-degree angle to each other, can capture a natural stereo image with minimal phase issues. The ORTF technique, which involves two mics placed 17 cm apart at a 110-degree angle, mimics the human ear and provides a spacious stereo image. The spaced pair technique, where two mics are placed several feet apart, can capture a wide and immersive sound but requires careful attention to phase alignment.

When it comes to mic placement, close-miking and room-miking offer different advantages. Close-miking involves placing the microphone very close to the sound source, capturing more direct sound and less room ambiance. This technique is useful in small spaces where room reflections can be problematic. Room-miking, on the other hand, involves placing the microphone farther away to capture the sound of the instrument along with the room's natural reverb. This technique can add depth and space to your recordings but might not be ideal in untreated or small rooms.

Each acoustic instrument requires specific techniques to capture its unique sound. For recording an acoustic guitar, avoid placing the mic directly in front of the sound hole as this can result in overwhelming bass frequencies. Instead, position the mic about 12 to 16 inches away from the 12th fret for a balanced sound that captures both the high-end sparkle and the body of the guitar. For a violin, capturing the bowing and resonance is crucial. Place a small diaphragm condenser mic about 18 inches above the instrument, angled towards the bridge. This position captures the richness of the violin's tone while minimizing bow noise. Recording a piano requires multiple mics for a balanced sound. Place one mic above the hammers and another near the soundboard to capture both the attack and resonance. For percussion, capturing the nuance of hand percussion and cymbals is key. Use a combination of close mics for detail and overhead mics for a full, balanced sound. Position the overhead mics in an XY or spaced pair configuration to capture the stereo image of the percussion setup.

Case Study: Recording an Acoustic Guitar in a Bedroom Studio

In a small bedroom studio, finding the right balance between capturing the guitar's natural sound and minimizing room reflections can be challenging. In one instance, a friend of ours used a combination of a large diaphragm condenser mic and a small diaphragm condenser mic to record an acoustic guitar. The large diaphragm condenser was positioned about 12 inches from the 12th fret, angled slightly towards the sound hole to capture the body of the guitar. The small diaphragm condenser was placed about 18 inches away, pointing towards the bridge to capture the high-end detail. This setup provided a balanced, full sound, highlighting the guitar's natural tone while minimizing room reflections.

In another example, different mic techniques were experimented with to achieve the desired sound. The XY technique was used to capture a natural stereo image, with two small diaphragm condensers placed at a 90-degree angle about 12 inches from the guitar. This technique provided a clear, focused sound with minimal phase issues. The spaced pair technique was also tried, with two mics placed several feet apart to capture a wider, more immersive sound. While this provided a rich stereo image, careful attention was needed to ensure phase alignment.

Recording acoustic instruments in a small space requires careful consideration of mic selection and placement. By understanding the challenges and applying the right techniques, you can achieve high-quality recordings that capture the essence of the instrument.

4.3 Direct Input (DI) Techniques for Electric Instruments

When we first started recording electric instruments at home, we quickly realized the benefits of using Direct Input (DI). Unlike mic'ing an amp, DI offers noise reduction and isolation, ensuring a cleaner signal. This method captures the instrument's sound without the interference of room acoustics or background noise. For many home setups, this can be a game-changer. A consistent, clean signal is easier to work with in post-production. It allows for greater flexibility in shaping the tone and applying effects. This is especially useful when not working with a perfectly treated room or high-quality amps.

Setting up DI for electric instruments is straightforward but varies slightly depending on the instrument. For electric guitars, a DI box is your best friend. Connect the guitar to the DI box using a standard instrument cable. Then, connect the DI box to your audio interface using an XLR cable. This setup ensures the signal is balanced and free from noise. Bass guitars benefit greatly from DI as well. The low-end clarity and punch you can achieve are remarkable. Connect the bass to the DI box and follow the same steps as for the electric guitar. Many audio interfaces also have built-in DI inputs, which can simplify the setup. For keyboards and synths, direct connection techniques are even simpler. These instruments typically have line-level outputs, so you can connect them directly to your audio interface using TRS or TS cables. This direct connection captures the full range of the instrument's sound, providing a clean slate for further processing.

Once you've captured a clean DI signal, the fun part begins—tone shaping and signal processing. Amp simulators and modeling software can transform a raw DI signal into a rich, dynamic sound. Software like AmpliTube or Guitar Rig offers a variety of virtual amps and effects. You can experiment with different amp models, speaker cabinets, and microphone placements, all within your DAW. This flexibility allows you to craft the perfect tone without needing multiple physical amps and pedals. Applying EQ and compression to DI signals can further enhance the sound. Use EQ to carve out unwanted frequencies and highlight the instrument's best qualities. For example, a slight boost around 3-5 kHz can add presence to a guitar track. Compression helps control the dynamics, ensuring a consistent level throughout the performance. This is particularly useful for bass guitars, where dynamic range can vary widely. Adding reverb and other effects can bring depth and character to your recordings. A touch of reverb can make a DI guitar sound like it's playing in a room or hall, adding a sense of space. Experiment with delay, chorus, and other effects to create unique textures and tones.

Troubleshooting DI recordings is essential to maintaining a high-quality signal. One common issue is ground loops, which can cause hum and noise. Using a DI box with a ground lift switch can eliminate this problem. Simply engage the ground lift switch to break the ground loop and reduce noise. Managing signal levels is also crucial to avoid clipping. Ensure your input levels are set correctly on both the DI box and audio interface. Aim for a strong signal without exceeding 0 dB to prevent distortion. Ensuring phase alignment with other recorded tracks is another important consideration. If you're blending DI signals with mic'd signals, phase issues can arise. Use a phase alignment tool or manually adjust the phase in your DAW to ensure the signals are in phase. This alignment will result in a fuller, more coherent sound.

Direct Input techniques offer a practical and efficient way to record electric instruments at home. By understanding the benefits, setting up correctly, and applying thoughtful processing, you can achieve professional-quality recordings. Whether you're working with guitars, basses, or synths, DI opens up a world of possibilities. It provides the flexibility and control needed to produce top-tier audio in any home environment.

With these recording techniques, you now have the tools to capture high-quality sound in various scenarios. From vocals and acoustic instruments to electric setups, each method enhances your home studio's potential. As we move forward, we'll dive into achieving professional sound quality, ensuring your recordings shine.

Chapter Five

Achieving Professional Sound Quality

We recall a particular session when we were recording a podcast at home and noticed a persistent hum in the background. No matter how much we adjusted our setup, the noise wouldn't go away. It wasn't until we delved deeper into noise reduction techniques that we managed to clean up our recordings. This chapter is dedicated to helping you achieve that same level of professional sound quality by eliminating unwanted noise from your home studio.

5.1 Noise Reduction Techniques for Home Studios

Noise is an inevitable part of any home recording environment. It can stem from various sources that you might not even consider initially. Background noise from household appliances like refrigerators, air conditioners, and computers can seep into your recordings. These subtle hums and whirs, though often quiet, become glaringly obvious on playback. External noise from traffic, neighbors, or even distant construction work can disrupt a clean recording session. Living in a busy neighborhood or near a main road can introduce unpredictable noise spikes. Additionally, room noise from HVAC systems and fans, often unnoticed in everyday life, can add an unwanted layer of sound to your tracks. These noises can muddy your recordings, making professional-quality audio difficult to achieve.

Minimizing noise at the source is your first line of defense. Using isolation shields and vocal booths can significantly reduce the intrusion of ambient noise. These tools create a controlled environment around your microphone, blocking out external sounds and reflections. Isolation shields, such as the SE Electronics Reflexion Filter, are portable and easy to set up around your mic, providing immediate noise reduction. Vocal booths, while more substantial, offer an even higher level of isolation. For instance, the VocalBoothTo-Go is a budget-friendly option many home studio enthusiasts prefer. Another practical tip is to choose quieter times for recording. Typically, late at night or early mornings are quieter, with less traffic and ambient noise. Scheduling your sessions during these times can greatly reduce the amount of background noise in your recordings. Implementing soundproofing techniques, such as adding weather stripping around doors and windows or hanging heavy curtains, can further isolate your recording space from external noise. Even simple measures like using a thick rug on the floor can absorb sound and reduce reflections.

Once you've minimized noise at the source, using noise reduction tools and software can clean up any remaining unwanted sounds in your recordings. Noise gates and ex-panders are effective tools for managing noise levels. A noise gate works by cutting off the audio signal when it falls below a certain threshold, effectively silencing the quieter, unwanted sounds. Expanders function similarly but with more subtlety, reducing the level of the noise rather than cutting it off entirely. Spectral editing tools, like those found in iZotope RX, allow you to visually identify and remove specific frequencies of noise. This can be particularly useful for eliminating hums and buzzes without affecting the rest of the audio. Popular noise reduction plugins, such as iZotope RX and Waves NS1, offer specialized algorithms to clean up your tracks. These plugins analyze the noise profile and intelligently reduce it, preserving the integrity of the original audio.

Step-by-Step Tutorials for Using Noise Reduction Tools

Setting up a noise gate for vocals can be straightforward with the right approach. Start by inserting a noise gate plugin on your vocal track. Set the threshold just above the noise floor, so the gate only opens when the vocal signal is present. Adjust the attack and release times to ensure the gate opens and closes smoothly, avoiding any abrupt cuts. This method can effectively reduce background noise during pauses in the vocal performance.

Using spectral editing to remove hums and buzzes involves a more detailed process. Open your audio file in a spectral editing tool like iZotope RX. Identify the frequency range of the hum or buzz by visually inspecting the spectrogram. Select the problematic frequencies and use the spectral repair tool to attenuate or remove them. This precise editing can clean up your track without affecting the desired audio components.

Applying noise reduction plugins to a mix is a powerful way to tackle persistent noise issues. Insert the noise reduction plugin on the track or the master bus. Begin by capturing a noise profile from a section of the audio that contains only the noise. The plugin then uses this profile to differentiate between the noise and the desired audio. Adjust the reduction amount to balance noise removal with maintaining audio quality. Plugins like iZotope RX Advanced offer detailed controls to fine-tune the process, ensuring a clean and professional result.

Achieving professional sound quality in your home studio is possible with the right techniques and tools. By identifying common noise sources, implementing practical noise reduction strategies, and utilizing advanced software, you can significantly enhance the clarity and quality of your recordings. This foundation will enable you to produce clean, professional audio, making your home studio a powerful space for creativity and production.

5.2 Effective EQ Settings for Various Instruments

Understanding the basics of EQ is crucial for shaping and enhancing the sound of different instruments in your mix. EQ, or equalization, allows you to adjust the balance between frequency components. The frequency spectrum is generally divided into lows, mids, and highs. Lows cover the bass frequencies, mids include the body and presence of the sound, and highs capture the brightness and clarity. Different types of EQ, such as parametric, graphic, and shelving, offer various ways to manipulate these frequencies. Parametric EQs provide precise control with adjustable frequency, gain, and Q factor (bandwidth). Graphic EQs have fixed frequency bands and sliders for adjustment. Shelving EQs boost or cut frequencies above or below a certain point, ideal for broad adjustments.

Applying EQ effectively can transform your recordings. For vocals, reducing muddiness and enhancing clarity is key. Start by cutting the low frequencies below 100 Hz with a high-pass filter to remove unwanted rumble. Boost around 2-4 kHz to add presence and intelligibility. If the vocals sound too harsh, a slight cut in the 5-8 kHz range can reduce sibilance. For acoustic guitars, adding warmth and sparkle makes them stand out. Cut around 100-250 Hz if the sound is too boomy. Boosting between 3-5 kHz can add brightness and bring out the picking details. A subtle lift around 10-12 kHz can add a touch of sparkle.

Drums require a different approach. For the kick drum, tightening the sound involves boosting the low end around 60-100 Hz for thump and adding a slight boost around 3-5 kHz for the attack. Cutting the mids around 250-500 Hz can reduce boxiness. The snare drum benefits from a boost in the 100-250 Hz range for body and 5-7 kHz for snap. Reducing frequencies around 800 Hz can clear up any muddiness. The bass guitar is the foundation of your low end. Defining it involves boosting the fundamental frequencies around 60-100 Hz and cutting the muddy mids around 200-500 Hz. Adding a slight boost around 1-2 kHz can help the bass cut through the mix without overpowering other elements.

Practical examples illustrate the impact of these EQ settings. Imagine a vocal track that sounds muffled and unclear. Applying a high-pass filter to remove low-end rumble and boosting around 3 kHz can make the vocals sound more present and clear. Similarly, an acoustic guitar track that lacks brightness can be transformed by cutting the boomy frequencies and boosting the highs. Before-and-after comparisons make these changes evident, showing how targeted EQ adjustments can enhance the overall sound.

Using EQ creatively allows you to shape your unique sound. Subtractive EQ, where you cut unwanted frequencies rather than boosting desired ones, can create space in the mix. For example, cutting the low mids in a guitar track can make room for the bass without boosting the bass itself. High-pass and low-pass filters are invaluable for clarity. Applying a high-pass filter to non-bass instruments removes unnecessary low frequencies, preventing them from muddying the mix. Conversely, a low-pass filter can remove unwanted high-frequency noise from bass instruments, focusing their energy in the low end.

Mid-range boosts can enhance presence and intelligibility. Boosting around 2-4 kHz on lead instruments or vocals can make them stand out in the mix. However, be cautious with these boosts to avoid harshness. Each instrument and mix is unique, requiring a tailored approach. Experiment with different settings and trust your ears. Reference tracks can guide you, providing a benchmark for achieving a balanced mix that translates well across different playback systems.

5.3 Balancing Levels for a Cohesive Mix

Balancing levels is crucial for creating a cohesive and professional-sounding mix. It allows each element in your mix to have its own space, ensuring clarity and separation between instruments. When levels are balanced correctly, you prevent masking, where one instrument overshadows another. This clarity helps each part of the mix stand out, making it easier for listeners to hear individual elements. Setting the right levels for different elements also ensures that no single part dominates the mix unless intended. A well-balanced mix is like a well-orchestrated piece of music where each instrument plays its role perfectly, contributing to the overall harmony.

To achieve a well-balanced mix, start with the foundational elements: drums and bass. These components form the backbone of most tracks, providing rhythm and groove. Begin by setting the levels for your kick drum and bass guitar. Ensure the kick is punchy and clear, sitting well in the low frequencies without overpowering the bass. Adjust the bass to complement the kick, making sure it's audible yet not overwhelming. Once the foundation is solid, bring in the snare drum and other drum elements. The snare should cut through the mix, providing a sharp and defined rhythm. Next, add in the melodic instruments like guitars and keyboards. These elements should sit above the rhythm section, adding texture and melody without clashing. Finally, introduce the vocals. Vocals should be prominent, sitting on top of the mix, but balanced enough to blend with the instruments harmoniously.

Effects and background elements add depth and dimension to your mix. Adjust the levels of reverb, delay, and other effects to enhance the overall sound without overshadowing the main elements. Background elements, such as ambient sounds or secondary instruments, should be audible but not distracting. They should add to the richness of the mix without drawing attention away from the primary instruments and vocals.

Visual aids and tools can be incredibly helpful in achieving balanced levels. VU meters and peak meters provide visual feedback on your levels, helping you ensure nothing is peaking or too quiet. VU meters show the average level of your signal, giving you an idea of perceived loudness, while peak meters display the instantaneous level, helping you avoid clipping. Using reference tracks can also guide you in setting levels. Listen to professionally mixed tracks in a similar genre and compare the levels of different elements. This comparison can help you achieve a similar balance in your mix. Plugins like iZotope Insight and Waves PAZ Analyzer offer advanced visual tools for level balancing. These plugins provide detailed metering, spectrum analysis, and loudness measurement, giving you comprehensive insights into your mix.

Maintaining balance throughout the mixing process requires ongoing attention. Regularly check your levels in different listening environments, such as studio monitors, headphones, and even car speakers. This practice ensures your mix translates well across various playback systems. Using automation to maintain balance is another effective strategy. Automate volume levels to ensure consistency throughout the track. For example, if a guitar solo gets too loud in one section, use automation to bring it down to a more appropriate level. Reassessing levels after applying effects is crucial. Effects like reverb and compression can alter the perceived loudness of elements. After adding these effects, revisit your levels to ensure nothing has become too loud or too quiet.

Balancing levels is an ongoing process that requires careful listening and adjustment. By starting with the foundational elements, gradually bringing in other parts, and using visual aids, you can achieve a cohesive and professional-sounding mix. Regularly checking your levels in different environments and using automation ensures a consistent mix that sounds great on any playback system. This foundation of a well-balanced mix will pave the way for more advanced techniques and creative decisions, setting the stage for mastering and final polishing in the next chapter.

Chapter Six

Developing Critical Listening Skills

The first time we heard a track we had mixed played back on a high-end sound system, we were floored. The nuances and details we thought we had captured were either missing or exaggerated. That moment made us realize the gap between what we thought we heard and what was actually there. This chapter is designed to bridge that gap for you, emphasizing the importance of developing critical listening skills to elevate your audio production capabilities.

6.1 Frequency Response: What to Listen For

Understanding frequency response is fundamental in audio production. Frequency response refers to how an audio system reproduces different frequencies. It's the range of frequencies that a piece of audio equipment can accurately reproduce. This concept is crucial because it affects how we perceive sound. Different frequencies contribute to the overall character and quality of the audio. Low frequencies, or bass, provide warmth and fullness. Mid frequencies, or mids, add presence and body. High frequencies, or treble, bring clarity and air. Knowing how to identify and manipulate these frequencies can significantly improve your mixes and recordings.

Low frequencies, ranging from 20 Hz to around 250 Hz, are the foundation of any mix. These frequencies add depth and weight to the sound. Bass and sub-bass frequencies fall within this range. They are responsible for the thump and rumble you feel in your chest when listening to music with a strong low end. Properly managing low frequencies is crucial. Too much bass can make a mix sound muddy, while too little can make it sound thin. Instruments like bass guitar, kick drums, and synth bass occupy this range. Ensuring they are balanced and clear is essential for a solid mix.

Mid frequencies, from 250 Hz to around 2.5 kHz, are where most of the audio content lives. This range includes the fundamental frequencies of many instruments and vocals. The mids contribute to the presence and body of the sound. They are crucial for clarity and definition. Vocals, guitars, pianos, and most other instruments have significant content in this range. Properly balancing the mids can make your mix sound full and rich. Too much emphasis on mid frequencies can make a mix sound boxy or honky, while too little can make it sound hollow.

High frequencies, from 2.5 kHz to around 20 kHz, add brightness and detail to the sound. They provide the clarity and air that make a mix sparkle. High frequencies include the overtones and harmonics of many instruments, adding texture and depth. Cymbals, hi-hats, and the sibilance in vocals are all found in this range. Managing high frequencies is about finding the right balance. Too much high end can make a mix sound harsh and fatiguing, while too little can make it sound dull and lifeless.

Practical listening exercises are invaluable for developing a keen ear for these frequencies. One effective exercise is using sine wave sweeps to identify frequencies. Play a sine wave that sweeps through the entire frequency spectrum, from 20 Hz to 20 kHz. Listen closely and note how different frequencies sound. This exercise helps you become familiar with the characteristics of various frequency ranges. Another exercise involves listening to isolated frequency bands in a mix. Use an EQ to solo different frequency ranges and listen to how each one contributes to the overall sound. This practice helps you understand the role of each frequency range in a mix. Comparing different EQ settings on the same track can also be enlightening. Apply various EQ adjustments to a track and listen to how each one affects the sound. This exercise trains your ear to hear the impact of specific frequency changes.

Improving your frequency response recognition requires regular practice. One effective method is regularly using reference tracks. Listen to professionally mixed and mastered tracks in the same genre as your work. Pay attention to how different frequency ranges are balanced. This practice helps you set a benchmark for your own mixes. Using quality monitoring equipment is also crucial. Accurate monitors and headphones allow you to hear the true representation of the audio. Investing in good monitoring gear ensures you make informed decisions based on accurate sound reproduction. Experimenting with EQ adjustments is another way to enhance your skills. Use EQ plugins to make subtle changes and listen to the results. This experimentation helps you understand the relationship between frequencies and their impact on the overall sound.

Developing critical listening skills is an ongoing journey. By understanding frequency response and practicing regularly, you can hone your ability to identify and manipulate different frequencies. This skill is essential for producing professional-quality audio, whether mixing, recording, or designing sound.

6.2 Identifying Common Mixing Problems by Ear

Mixing a track can sometimes feel like solving a complex puzzle. One of the most common issues you'll encounter is a muddy mix. This happens when there are excess low frequencies, causing a lack of clarity. It often sounds like everything is crowded in the lower end, making it hard to distinguish between instruments. You might notice the kick drum and bass guitar fighting for space, leading to a boomy or indistinct sound.

Another frequent problem is harshness and sibilance. This occurs when there are overly bright high frequencies, producing piercing sounds that can be unpleasant to listen to. Harshness typically affects instruments like cymbals and high-hats, while sibilance impacts vocals, making "s" and "sh" sounds overly pronounced. Listening to a mix with harshness can be fatiguing, and it often results in listeners wanting to turn down the volume.

Frequency masking is a more subtle yet equally problematic issue. It happens when instruments clash in the same frequency range, causing them to mask each other. For example, a vocal might get lost when it shares the same midrange frequencies as a guitar. This makes it hard to hear each element clearly, leading to a flat and congested mix where important details are lost.

Imbalance in levels is another common mixing problem. This is when one element dominates the mix while others are too quiet. You might find a snare drum that is too loud, overshadowing the vocals, or a guitar that is buried beneath other instruments. This imbalance can disrupt the overall harmony and make the mix sound unprofessional.

Recognizing these issues by ear involves careful listening and a keen awareness of how different problems manifest. A muddy mix will sound crowded and unclear, lacking definition in the low end. Harshness will present as a sharp, grating sound in the high frequencies, often causing discomfort. Frequency masking makes it difficult to pick out individual instruments, as they seem to blend into each other. An imbalance in levels is more straightforward to identify, as you'll notice certain elements overpowering others.

Practical listening exercises are invaluable for honing your ability to identify these problems. Start by analyzing poorly mixed tracks to identify specific issues. Listen to tracks that suffer from muddiness, harshness, masking, and imbalance. Take notes on what you hear and try to pinpoint the exact problems. Comparing problematic mixes with well-balanced ones can also be enlightening. By listening to a well-mixed track immediately after a poorly mixed one, the differences become more apparent. This exercise helps you develop an ear for what a good mix should sound like.

Using spectral analyzers can provide a visual representation of what you're hearing. These tools display the frequency content of your audio, helping you see where problems might lie. For instance, if you notice a buildup of low frequencies on the analyzer, it can confirm a muddy mix. Correlating what you see with what you hear reinforces your ability to identify issues by ear.

Once you've identified common mixing problems, addressing them involves specific techniques. To reduce muddiness, use EQ to cut excess low frequencies. Apply a high-pass filter to instruments that don't need low-end content, like vocals and guitars. This clears up space for the bass and kick drum. To tackle harshness, use a parametric EQ to identify and reduce the offending high frequencies. A de-esser plugin can be particularly effective for managing sibilance in vocals, targeting the specific frequency range where the problem lies.

Addressing frequency masking involves both EQ and panning. Use EQ to carve out space for each instrument by reducing overlapping frequencies. For example, if a vocal and guitar clash in the midrange, cut the mid frequencies in the guitar to make room for the vocal. Panning instruments to different positions in the stereo field can also help separate them, reducing masking and enhancing clarity.

Imbalance in levels can be corrected through careful adjustment and multiband compression. Start by setting the levels of your foundational elements, like drums and bass. Gradually bring in other elements, adjusting their levels to achieve a balanced mix. Multiband compression can control dynamic range issues within specific frequency bands, ensuring no single element dominates the mix.

Developing your critical listening skills takes time and practice. By regularly identifying and addressing common mixing problems, you'll improve your ability to create professional-quality mixes that stand out.

6.3 Critical Listening Exercises with Downloadable Samples

Your ability to listen critically is one of the most valuable skills you can develop in audio production. Regular practice can enhance your listening skills and overall audio production quality. Building a critical ear takes time, but the payoff is significant. When you train your ears, you reinforce theoretical knowledge with practical application. This process helps you recognize subtle nuances in audio, making you a better producer, engineer, and musician.

To facilitate this practice, we've included a variety of downloadable audio samples. These samples are designed to provide hands-on experience with different aspects of critical listening. You'll find isolated instrument tracks, which allow you to focus on individual elements without the distraction of a full mix. This isolation helps you understand how each instrument should sound in detail. Additionally, there are full mixes with intentional issues. These mixes are created to help you identify and correct common problems, such as muddiness or harshness. Finally, reference tracks are included for comparison. These tracks are professionally mixed and mastered, providing a benchmark for you to aim for in your own work.

One of the most effective ways to improve your critical listening skills is through structured exercises. Start by identifying frequency ranges in isolated tracks. Play a track and focus on the different frequency bands. Use an EQ plugin to solo each band and listen carefully to how it affects the sound. This exercise helps you become familiar with the characteristics of various frequencies and how they contribute to the overall mix. Another valuable exercise is spotting mixing issues in the provided samples. Listen to the full mixes with intentional problems and try to identify what's wrong. Is there too much bass? Are the vocals too harsh? This practice trains your ear to recognize issues quickly and accurately.

Comparing your mixes to high-quality reference tracks is another powerful exercise. Load a reference track into your DAW and switch between it and your mix. Listen for differences in balance, clarity, and overall sound quality. This comparison helps you understand what a professional mix should sound like and identify areas where your mix falls short. Analyzing the impact of different effects and processing techniques is also crucial. Apply various effects, such as reverb or compression, to a track and listen to how they change the sound. Experiment with different settings and note the results. This hands-on approach helps you understand how to use these tools effectively.

To aid in your critical listening practice, we recommend using specific tools and software. Spectrum analyzers and visual EQ plugins provide visual feedback on your audio, helping you see what you're hearing. These tools can confirm what you identify by ear, reinforcing your listening skills. A/B comparison tools are also invaluable. They allow you to quickly switch between two audio sources, making it easier to compare your mix to a reference track or different versions of your mix. Software for creating and managing listening exercises can streamline your practice. Programs like SoundGym offer ear training exercises tailored for audio professionals, helping you develop your skills in a structured and efficient way.

The importance of critical listening cannot be overstated. Regular practice with dedicated exercises can significantly enhance your ability to produce high-quality audio. By using the provided samples and recommended tools, you can develop a keen ear and a deep understanding of audio production. This skill set is essential for achieving professional results and standing out in a competitive field.

In this chapter, we've explored the importance of developing critical listening skills and provided practical exercises to enhance your abilities. By regularly practicing with the downloadable samples and utilizing the recommended tools, you'll build a critical ear that will elevate your audio production quality. This foundation will serve you well as we move into the next chapter, where we'll dive into creative sound design techniques to further expand your skill set.

Chapter Seven

Creative Sound Design

We remember the first time we experimented with effects in our home studio. We had a simple vocal track that sounded flat and lifeless. Out of curiosity, we added a touch of reverb, and suddenly, the vocal took on a new dimension. It was as if the voice was transported into a grand cathedral, echoing with richness and depth. That moment opened our eyes to the transformative power of effects in sound design. Effects are not just tools for fixing problems; they are powerful creative instruments that can turn ordinary sounds into extraordinary ones.

Using Effects to Create Unique Sounds

The role of effects in sound design is akin to a painter's brush strokes on a canvas. Effects like reverb, delay, modulation, and distortion can dramatically alter the character of a sound, adding depth, movement, and texture. Reverb simulates the way sound reflects and decays in different spaces, from small rooms to vast halls. Delay creates echoes, adding rhythm and complexity. Modulation effects such as chorus, flanger, and phaser introduce movement and width, making sounds more dynamic and engaging. Distortion adds grit and intensity, transforming clean sounds into something raw and powerful.

The traditional applications of these effects are well-known, but their creative uses extend far beyond standard practices. Reverb can be used to place a sound in a virtual space and create otherworldly textures. For instance, applying severe pitch correction before reverb can yield robotic, metallic sounds, which is perfect for sci-fi projects. Reverse reverb, where you reverse a track, apply reverb, and then reverse it back, creates an ethereal, swelling effect often used on vocals and cymbals. Sidechaining reverb to an instrument can produce a pumping effect, adding a rhythmic pulse commonly found in EDM. Automating reverb parameters like size, panning, and filtering in real time can evolve a static sound into a dynamic, ever-changing sonic landscape.

Delay, too, offers more than just echoes. By manipulating delay times and feedback settings, you can create intricate rhythmic patterns that add syncopation and complexity to a track. For example, setting a delay to a dotted eighth note can introduce a driving, rhythmic feel that complements the main beat. Combining reverb and delay can expand the spatial effects, creating lush, immersive environments. This technique is particularly effective in ambient music, where the interplay between delayed echoes and reverb tails can form vast, dreamy soundscapes.

Modulation effects bring a unique flair to sound design, adding movement and interest. Chorus and flanger effects can widen and thicken sounds, making them feel more expansive. A chorus effect, for instance, can make a single vocal or guitar track sound like a rich, multi-layered ensemble. Flanger creates swirling, jet-like textures, perfect for adding a psychedelic touch to synths or guitars. Phaser effects introduce phase shifts, resulting in a sweeping, dynamic texture that can add depth and intrigue to pads and leads. Tremolo and vibrato effects modulate amplitude and pitch, respectively, adding rhythmic modulation that can enhance the groove and feel of a track.

Practical Examples and Sound Clips

Consider transforming a vocal track with heavy reverb and delay. Start with a dry vocal recording and apply a long, lush reverb to create a sense of space. Next, add a delay set to a rhythmic value that complements the tempo of the song. Adjust the feedback to create a cascading echo effect. The result is a vocal that feels expansive and immersive as if it were recorded in a grand hall with natural echoes.

Using modulation effects on synth pads can create evolving textures that keep the listener engaged. Apply a chorus effect to widen the sound and add depth. Layer a flanger effect to introduce movement and a sense of motion. Finally, add a phaser with slow modulation to create a swirling, dynamic texture. This combination transforms a simple synth pad into a rich, evolving soundscape that feels alive and constantly changing.

Creating a sense of space in ambient recordings often involves layering reverb and delay. Start with a field recording, such as the sound of rain or a distant cityscape. Apply a long reverb to place the recording in a vast, open space. Add a delay with a high feedback setting to create echoes that blend into the reverb tail. This technique creates an immersive, atmospheric recording that transports the listener to another place.

By exploring the creative potential of effects, you can transform ordinary sounds into unique, captivating audio experiences. Whether you're working with vocals, synths, or ambient recordings, the right combination of effects can elevate your sound design to new heights. Experiment with different settings, trust your ears and let your creativity guide you.

Layering and Texturing Audio

Layering in sound design is like building a sonic tapestry. By combining multiple sound sources, you can create rich, complex textures that a single sound could never achieve. Imagine a simple synth pad. By itself, it might sound thin and uninspiring. But layer it with a deep bass, some airy noise, and a few organic elements, and suddenly, you have a sound that feels full and dynamic. Layering allows you to fill out the frequency spectrum, ensuring that no part of your mix feels empty or lacking. Each layer can occupy a different part of the spectrum, from the low rumbles of a bass to the high shimmers of a cymbal, creating a balanced and immersive sound.

Effective audio layering requires a strategic approach. One method is to combine synthesized and organic sounds. Synthesized sounds provide precision and control, while organic sounds add warmth and realism. For example, layering a synthesized drone with the sound of rustling leaves can create a more engaging and lifelike texture. Using different frequency ranges for each layer is also crucial. You don't want all your layers to occupy the same frequency range, as this can lead to a muddy mix. Instead, assign each layer a specific range. For instance, let the bass handle the low frequencies, the synth pad cover the mids, and the noise layer fill in the highs. This way, each layer has its own space to shine.

Blending transient and sustained elements can add further depth and interest. Transient elements, like a snare hit or a plucked string, provide sharp, clear attacks that add definition to your sound. Sustained elements, like a long reverb tail or a continuous pad, fill in the gaps, creating a sense of continuity and flow. By combining these two types of elements, you can create punchy and smooth sounds, providing a more engaging listening experience.

Adding texture to your sounds makes them more interesting and engaging. Noise and ambiance layers are great for this purpose. A subtle layer of white noise or environmental sounds can add a sense of space and realism. Granular synthesis is another powerful tool for creating complex textures. This technique involves breaking a sound into tiny grains and manipulating them to create entirely new textures. For example, you could take a recording of a bell and use granular synthesis to stretch and morph it into an evolving pad. Incorporating field recordings can also add organic elements to your sound design. Recordings of natural environments, cityscapes, or even household objects can bring a unique character to your work.

Practical Exercises and Examples

Let's dive into some practical exercises to get your hands dirty with layering and texturing. Start by creating a layered pad sound using synths and samples. Choose a basic synth pad as your foundation. Add a deep bass layer to provide warmth and weight. Next, layer in some airy noise to fill out the high frequencies. Finally, add an organic element, like a field recording of wind or water, to give the pad a natural, evolving texture. Adjust the levels and EQ each layer to ensure they blend seamlessly.

Designing a textured sound effect for multimedia involves similar techniques. Suppose you're creating a sound for a magical spell in a video game. Start with a synthesized whoosh as the base layer. Add sparkles or chimes for the high frequencies, giving the spell a magical feel. Layer in a deep rumble or sub-bass to add power and impact. Finally, incorporate some field recordings, like the crackling of fire or the rustle of leaves, to add realism and depth. This combination of synthesized and organic elements can create a rich, immersive sound effect that enhances the visual experience.

Layering percussion elements can create a fuller, more dynamic sound. Start with a basic drum loop as your foundation. Add a layer of hand percussion, like shakers or tambourines, to introduce some high-frequency texture. Layer in a low-frequency element, like a sub kick or a tom, to add weight and depth. Finally, incorporate some background ambiance, like crowd noise or environmental sounds, to give the percussion a sense of space and context. This approach can transform a simple drum loop into a complex, engaging rhythm section.

By mastering the techniques of layering and texturing, you can elevate your sound design to new heights. Whether you're creating music, sound effects, or ambient recordings, these skills will enable you to craft rich, immersive audio experiences that captivate and engage your audience.

Sound Design for Film and Games

Sound design for film and games has its unique set of requirements that set it apart from music production. In these media, synchronization with visual elements is paramount. Every sound must align perfectly with the on-screen action to maintain the illusion of reality. For example, the sound of footsteps must match the character's steps, and the roar of an engine should sync with the car's movement. This level of synchronization helps to create immersive environments that draw the audience into the story or gameplay, making them feel as if they are part of the action.

Creating impactful sound effects for film and games involves a blend of technical skill and creativity. Foley techniques are essential for producing realistic sound effects. Foley artists use everyday objects to replicate sounds that match the visual elements on screen. For instance, the sound of a character walking on gravel can be recreated by crushing small stones underfoot in a controlled environment. This method ensures the sound is clear and perfectly timed with the visual.

Synthesis can be a powerful tool for sci-fi and fantasy projects. Using synthesizers, you can create sounds that don't exist in the real world, such as the hum of a futuristic space-ship or the roar of a mythical creature. Layering and processing these synthetic sounds can add depth and cinematic impact. For example, a laser blast might combine a synthesized high-pitched tone with a deep, rumbling bass layer to create a rich, multi-dimensional sound. This layering technique makes the sound more engaging and ensures it stands out in the mix, even during high-action scenes.

Ambience and background sounds play a crucial role in setting the tone and atmosphere in film and games. Designing ambient soundscapes involves creating a backdrop that enhances the visual setting without drawing attention away from the main action. For instance, a forest scene might include layers of birdsong, rustling leaves, and distant water streams. Using field recordings can add authenticity to these ambient sounds. Capturing real-world sounds and incorporating them into your project can provide a sense of realism that synthetic sounds might lack.

Looping and layering techniques are also vital for creating seamless background sounds. By carefully looping ambient sounds, you can ensure they play continuously without noticeable breaks or repetitions. Layering different ambient elements at varying volumes and frequencies can create a rich, immersive soundscape that feels natural and all-encompassing. This approach is particularly effective in video games, where the player's environment constantly shifts and evolves.

Case Study: Sound Design for a Short Film

In a recent short film project, we were tasked with creating the sound design for a suspenseful night-time forest scene. The goal was to build tension and immerse the audience in the eerie atmosphere. We started with field recordings of night-time forest sounds, capturing crickets, distant owls, and the rustling of leaves. These recordings formed the base layer of the ambient soundscape.

Next, we added Foley effects to match the character's movements. Every twig snap and footstep was meticulously recorded in a controlled environment to ensure clarity and synchronization. To enhance the suspense, we used synthesis to create a low, rumbling drone that subtly increased in volume as the scene progressed. This drone added an underlying sense of unease without overpowering the ambient sounds.

In a game environment, sound design requires a different approach due to the interactive nature of the medium. For example, in an action-adventure game, we created a library of sound effects for various actions, such as sword swings, magical spells, and environmental interactions. Each sound had to be distinct and impactful to ensure the player received immediate auditory feedback for their actions.

Designing an ambient soundscape for a film scene involved a similar process. In a scene set in a bustling marketplace, we layered field recordings of crowd chatter, distant street musicians, and the clinking of coins. By carefully balancing these elements, we created a vibrant, dynamic background that brought the scene to life.

Understanding the unique requirements and techniques of sound design for film and games allows you to create immersive, engaging audio experiences. Each project may demand different approaches, but the principles of synchronization, creativity, and authenticity remain constant. By mastering these techniques, you can elevate your sound design and bring any visual story to life.

Chapter Eight

Mixing Techniques

We remember the first time we experienced a song that felt like it was coming from all around me, with instruments perfectly placed in the stereo field. It was a revelation. The mix had so much depth and clarity, and each element had its own space. That's when we realized the power of panning. This chapter focuses on how you can use panning to create a wide, immersive soundstage in your mixes.

8.1 Panning Strategies for a Wide Soundstage

Panning is a crucial aspect of mixing that contributes significantly to the spatial dimension and clarity of your mix. By strategically placing sounds within the stereo field, you can create separation between instruments, enhancing the overall stereo image. This separation helps avoid frequency masking, where similar frequencies clash and make it difficult to distinguish individual elements. For example, placing a guitar on the left and a keyboard on the right can prevent them from stepping on each other's toes, allowing each instrument to shine.

Effective panning can make your mix sound wider and more immersive. Hard-panning, where an instrument is placed fully to the left or right, can create a dramatic sense of space. This technique works well for doubled instruments, like heavy electric guitars or synths, making the mix sound fuller. Subtle panning, on the other hand, involves placing instruments slightly off-center, creating a more natural and less exaggerated stereo image. This method is useful for elements like backing vocals or percussive layers, adding width without overwhelming the listener.

Panning rhythm and lead elements differently is another effective strategy. For instance, you can center the kick, snare, and bass to provide a solid foundation, while panning hi-hats, toms, and cymbals to the sides to create a sense of width. Lead elements, such as vocals or solo instruments, often stay centered to keep the focus. However, adding a touch of automated panning to these elements can create movement and keep the listener engaged. For example, a subtle left-to-right pan on a guitar solo can add excitement and make the section stand out.

Different instruments require unique panning approaches to achieve optimal placement in a mix. Drums and percussion benefit from thoughtful panning to replicate the experience of a live performance. For a natural feel, pan the drum kit to mimic the drummer's perspective: hi-hat slightly to the left, toms spread across the stereo field, and cymbals panned wide. This approach creates a realistic and immersive drum sound.

Guitars and keyboards can be panned to create a balanced and wide mix. If you have multiple guitar tracks, consider panning them opposite each other to create a stereo spread. For example, pan one rhythm guitar hard left and another hard right. This technique, known as complementary panning, helps prevent frequency clashes and gives the mix a full, rich sound. Keyboards can be panned similarly, with different parts spread across the stereo field to create a spacious and dynamic mix.

Vocals and harmonies often take center stage, but that doesn't mean they should be limited to the middle of the stereo field. Main vocals typically stay centered to maintain focus, but background harmonies can be panned to create a sense of space and depth. For instance, pan harmonies slightly left and right to surround the lead vocal, adding dimension without drawing attention away from the main performance.

Practical Exercise: Mastering Panning Techniques

To practice panning techniques, start with a drum kit. Load a drum loop into your DAW and pan the elements to create a natural feel. Place the kick and snare in the center, hi-hat slightly left, toms across the stereo field, and cymbals wide. Listen to how the panning affects the overall sound and make adjustments as needed.

Next, try creating a wide guitar sound with double tracking. Record the same guitar part twice and pan one track hard left and the other hard right. Notice how this creates a fuller and more immersive sound. You can apply the same technique to keyboards or any other doubled instruments.

Finally, experiment with panning automation for dynamic effects. Take a lead instrument, like a guitar solo, and automate the panning to move subtly from left to right. This movement can add excitement and keep the listener engaged. Be careful not to overdo it; subtlety is key to maintaining a professional sound.

By mastering these panning strategies, you can create wide, clear, and immersive mixes. Panning enhances the stereo image and helps each element find its own space, resulting in a more balanced and professional mix.

8.2 Using Compression to Control Dynamics

Compression is a powerful tool in the mixing process, helping you manage dynamic range and enhance the overall mix. It smooths out volume inconsistencies, ensuring that softer parts are audible and louder parts are controlled. This creates a more balanced and cohesive sound. Compression also adds punch and sustain to instruments, making drums hit harder, and guitars ring longer. By controlling peaks, it prevents clipping, which can distort the audio and ruin a mix. Proper use of compression can elevate a mix from amateur to professional, giving it a polished and consistent feel.

To use compression effectively, start by setting the threshold and ratio. The threshold determines the level at which compression kicks in. Signals above this level will be compressed, while those below remain unaffected. The ratio controls how much compression is applied. A ratio of 2:1 means that for every 2 dB above the threshold, the output increases by only 1 dB. This subtle compression can smooth out minor inconsistencies. For more aggressive control, higher ratios like 4:1 or 8:1 are useful. However, be careful not to over-compress, as this can squash the dynamics and make the mix sound lifeless.

Adjusting the attack and release times is crucial for shaping the character of the compression. Attack time determines how quickly the compressor responds to signals above the threshold. Fast attack times catch transients and reduce peaks, but can also dull the sound. Slow attack times let transients pass through, adding punch to drums and percussive elements. Release time controls how quickly the compressor stops reducing gain after the signal falls below the threshold. A quick release can make the compression more noticeable, while a slower release smooths out the effect. Finding the right balance between attack and release times is key to achieving natural-sounding compression.

Sidechain compression is a creative technique that can add a dynamic element to your mix. This involves using the signal from one track to control the compression on another.

A common example is sidechaining the kick drum to the bass. When the kick hits, it ducks the bass slightly, creating space for the kick to punch through the mix. This technique is widely used in electronic music to create a pumping effect, but it can be applied to any genre to enhance clarity and separation between elements.

Different instruments benefit from specific compression settings to achieve the desired results. For vocals, compression ensures consistency and presence. Set a moderate threshold and a ratio of around 3:1 to smooth out volume fluctuations. Use a medium attack time to preserve the natural transients and a fast release to maintain a natural sound. This keeps the vocals upfront and clear without sounding over-processed. For drums, parallel compression can add punch without sacrificing dynamics. Create a duplicate of the drum bus and compress it heavily with a high ratio and fast attack and release times. Blend this compressed signal with the uncompressed drums to add weight and impact while retaining the original dynamics.

Bass dynamics can be controlled effectively with multi-band compression. This type of compression allows you to apply different settings to different frequency bands. For bass, you might want to compress the low frequencies more aggressively to keep them tight and controlled, while applying lighter compression to the mid and high frequencies. Set the threshold and ratio for each band according to the needs of the mix. This technique ensures a balanced and powerful bass sound that sits well in the mix without overpowering other elements.

Practical Examples and Settings

Let's start with vocal compression for a pop mix. Set the threshold so that the compressor engages on the louder parts of the performance. Use a ratio of around 3:1, a medium attack time, and a fast release. This setup smooths out the performance, keeping the vocals consistent and present without sounding unnatural. For drum bus compression, set a higher ratio, around 4:1, with a fast attack and release. This adds punch and tightness to the overall drum sound. Using a multi-band compressor on a bass track involves setting different thresholds and ratios for low, mid, and high frequencies. Compress the low end more heavily to control the bass's foundation while applying lighter compression to the mids and highs to retain their natural character.

By mastering these compression techniques, you can control the dynamics of your mix, adding punch, clarity, and consistency. Whether you're working with vocals, drums, or bass, understanding how to apply compression effectively will elevate your mixes to a professional level.

8.3 Advanced Reverb Techniques

Reverb plays a fundamental role in creating space within a mix. It adds depth and dimension, allowing each element to sit naturally within the stereo field. By simulating different acoustic environments, reverb can make a vocal track feel like it was recorded in a cathedral or a drum kit sound as if it were played in a spacious studio. This sense of space and depth helps blend elements into a cohesive mix, ensuring nothing sounds out of place or overly dry.

Using reverb creatively can elevate your mix from good to extraordinary. One advanced technique is utilizing pre-delay to create separation between the direct sound and the reverb. Pre-delay is the time between the initial sound and the onset of the reverb. By adjusting this, you can ensure the original signal remains clear before the reverb kicks in, adding clarity and definition. This is particularly useful on vocals, where you want the words to be intelligible but still surrounded by a lush reverb.

Layering different types of reverb can also create unique textures and spaces. For instance, combining a short plate reverb with a long hall reverb can add both immediacy and depth to a snare drum. The plate reverb provides a quick, bright reflection, while the hall reverb adds a tail that lingers, creating a rich and complex sound. Similarly, using a convolution reverb to simulate a real space, followed by a digital reverb for additional color, can create incredibly realistic and immersive environments.

Creating reverb tails for atmospheric effects is another powerful technique. By isolating a portion of the reverb tail and extending it, you can create pads or ambient layers that add a sense of space and movement. This technique works well in genres like ambient or cinematic music, where space and texture are crucial elements. Adjusting the tail's length and decay can transform a simple reverb into an evolving soundscape.

Reverb settings need to be tailored to different instruments to achieve the best results. For vocals, adding a subtle reverb can make them sound more natural and less dry. A short plate or room reverb with a moderate pre-delay can add a sense of space without overwhelming the vocal clarity. On snare drums, using a plate reverb can add character and energy. The bright reflections of a plate reverb enhance the snare's snap, making it more present in the mix. For strings, applying a hall reverb can create a lush and expansive sound. The long decay and rich reflections of a hall reverb can make strings sound grand and enveloping, perfect for orchestral or cinematic arrangements.

Practical Example: Designing a Reverb-Heavy Ambient Track

To illustrate these techniques, let's consider designing a reverb-heavy ambient track. Start with a vocal reverb chain that includes multiple stages. Begin with a short room reverb to add immediate space, followed by a longer hall reverb to create depth. Use pre-delay on the hall reverb to maintain vocal clarity. Next, apply a convolution reverb to a piano track to simulate a real space, like a concert hall. Follow this with a digital reverb for additional color and texture. Finally, create reverb tails for atmospheric effects by isolating and extending the tail of a synth pad. Adjust the decay and length to create an evolving soundscape that adds movement and space to the track.

Reverb is not just about making things sound bigger; it's about placing sounds in a natural and immersive space. By experimenting with different types of reverb, adjusting settings to suit each element, and using advanced techniques like pre-delay and reverb tails, you can create rich, deep, and full of character mixes.

When used thoughtfully, reverb can transform your mix, adding depth and cohesion. The techniques discussed here, from pre-delay to layering different types of reverb, provide a toolkit for creating immersive soundscapes. As you apply these methods, remember to listen critically and adjust settings to suit the unique needs of each mix. With practice, you'll find the perfect balance that brings your audio to life.

Chapter Nine

Mastering Audio

We will never forget the first time we listened to a track we'd mixed and then sent off to be mastered. When it came back, it was like hearing it for the first time. The depth, clarity, and punch were all enhanced, making the track sound complete. we realized then that a well-prepared mix is the foundation for effective mastering. Without a solid mix, no amount of mastering can save the track. This chapter will guide you through the essential steps to prepare your mix for mastering, ensuring your music reaches its full potential.

9.1 Preparing Your Mix for Mastering

A well-prepared mix sets the stage for effective mastering. It ensures that the levels and frequencies are balanced and that there is enough headroom for mastering adjustments. Balanced levels mean that no single element overpowers the others. This balance allows the mastering engineer to apply processing uniformly without having to fix mix-related issues. Ensuring that frequencies are well-distributed across the spectrum prevents any frequency from dominating the mix, which can lead to a muddy or harsh final product. Avoiding over-compression and excessive limiting during mixing is crucial. These processes should be gentle to maintain dynamics and leave room for mastering. Over-compressing can squash the track, making it sound lifeless and flat. Lastly, leaving headroom—typically around 2 to 3 dB—ensures that the mastering engineer has the space to apply final adjustments without causing distortion.

When it comes to exporting your final mix, there are several key steps to follow. First, set the correct bit depth and sample rate. Professional mastering typically requires a bit depth of 24 bits and a sample rate of 48 kHz or higher. This ensures that the audio quality remains high throughout the mastering process. Using lossless formats like WAV or AIFF is essential. These formats maintain the integrity of your audio, unlike compressed formats such as MP3, which can degrade quality. Ensuring proper labeling and organization of files is also crucial. Clearly label each file with the track name, bit depth, sample rate, and any other relevant information. This helps the mastering engineer understand the specifications of your mix and ensures a smooth workflow.

Creating a mastering session in your DAW involves several steps. Start by importing the final mix into a new session. This keeps the mastering process separate from the mixing process, allowing you to focus solely on mastering. Organize your tracks and sections logically. For instance, if you're mastering an album, arrange the tracks in the order they will appear. This helps you understand the flow and dynamics of the entire project. Setting up a reference track for comparison is highly beneficial. Choose a professionally mastered track in a similar genre and instrumentation. This reference track serves as a benchmark, allowing you to compare and ensure that your master meets industry standards. Tools like Adaptr Audio's Metric AB can be useful for easy A/B comparisons.

Critical listening before mastering is non-negotiable. It's essential to evaluate your mix thoroughly to identify any issues that need addressing before mastering. Listen to your mix in different environments—studio monitors, headphones, car speakers, and even consumer-grade earbuds. This helps you understand how your mix translates across various playback systems. Taking breaks during this process is vital to avoid ear fatigue. Continuous listening can dull your senses, leading to poor decision-making. Short breaks help reset your ears, allowing you to listen with fresh perspective. Making notes on areas that need attention is also helpful. Jot down any issues you notice, such as imbalances, harsh frequencies, or lack of clarity. Addressing these issues before mastering ensures a smoother process and a better final product.

To sum up, preparing your mix for mastering involves ensuring balanced levels and frequencies, avoiding over-compression, leaving headroom, exporting correctly, setting up a dedicated mastering session, and critically evaluating your mix. Each step is crucial in laying the foundation for effective mastering. By following these guidelines, you ensure that your music is ready to be polished to perfection, achieving the professional sound you're aiming for.

9.2 Essential Mastering Techniques

Mastering is the final step in the audio production process, where the primary goal is to polish the mix and prepare it for distribution. This involves several key processes: EQ adjustments for tonal balance, compression for dynamic consistency, and limiting to maximize loudness. Each of these techniques contributes to enhancing the overall sound quality and ensuring that the track translates well across various playback systems.

EQ adjustments are fundamental in mastering. They help achieve tonal balance by addressing any frequency imbalances present in the mix. The first step is to identify problematic frequencies. For instance, if the mix sounds too muddy, it might have excessive low frequencies that need to be reduced. Conversely, if it sounds harsh, there could be too much high-end that requires taming. Using gentle, broad EQ curves is crucial in mastering. Unlike mixing, where surgical EQ cuts and boosts are common, mastering requires subtler adjustments to avoid altering the mix's character. Apply wide Q settings to make smooth, natural-sounding changes. Mid/side EQ is another powerful tool in mastering. It allows you to process the mid (center) and side (stereo) components of the mix separately. For example, you can enhance the stereo width by boosting the high frequencies on the sides or bring more clarity to the vocals by cutting muddy frequencies in the center.

Compression in mastering is about controlling dynamics without compromising the mix's integrity. The goal is to achieve a consistent level throughout the track while preserving its natural dynamics. Start by setting the threshold, which determines at what level compression kicks in. Set the ratio for subtle compression, typically between 1.5:1 and 2:1. This gentle approach ensures that the compression enhances the mix without making it sound overly compressed. Adjusting the attack and release times is critical for transparency. A slower attack time allows transients to pass through, preserving the punch of the mix. A faster release time helps the compressor recover quickly, maintaining a natural sound. Multi-band compression is another technique used in mastering. It allows you to apply compression to specific frequency bands independently. This targeted control can help tighten the low end, smooth out the mids, and add shine to the highs, all without affecting the overall balance of the mix.

Effective limiting is essential for achieving competitive loudness levels. A limiter is a specialized compressor with a high ratio, usually set to prevent the signal from exceeding a specified ceiling. Start by setting the ceiling to just below 0 dBFS to prevent clipping and digital distortion. Using a look-ahead feature can enhance precision limiting, allowing the limiter to anticipate and react to peaks more effectively. This results in a smoother, more transparent limiting process. Balancing loudness with dynamic range preservation is crucial. While it's tempting to push the limiter hard to achieve maximum loudness, this can squash the dynamics and make the track sound flat. Aim to find a balance where the track is loud but still retains its dynamic range. This ensures that the mix remains engaging and musical.

Mastering is both a technical and an artistic process. It requires a deep understanding of how each technique affects the overall sound. By using EQ to balance the tonal spectrum, compression to control dynamics, and limiting to achieve the desired loudness, you can elevate your mix to a professional level. Each step should be approached with the intent to enhance the mix rather than to fix issues that should have been addressed during mixing. This mindset ensures that your mastering process will bring out the best in your music, making it ready for the world to hear.

9.3 Creating a Master that Translates Across Systems

One of the most critical aspects of mastering is ensuring that your track sounds good on various playback systems. You've likely spent hours perfecting your mix, but if it doesn't translate well across different speakers and headphones, all that effort can be in vain. The goal is to achieve consistency, so your music retains its quality whether it's played on high-end studio monitors, consumer headphones, or car speakers. This involves balancing frequencies so no particular range dominates on any system, ensuring the mix holds up in different environments.

To check how your master translates, it's essential to listen on multiple playback systems. Start with your studio monitors, as they provide the most accurate representation of your mix. Next, switch to headphones—both high-quality and consumer-grade—to catch any issues that might not be apparent on monitors. Finally, play your track on consumer speakers, like those in a living room or a car. Each environment reveals different aspects of your mix, and it's crucial to ensure your track sounds balanced and impactful in all of them.

Using reference tracks is another effective method for checking consistency. Choose a professionally mastered track in a similar genre and instrumentation. Compare your master to this reference track to identify any discrepancies in balance, clarity, or loudness. This comparison helps you understand how your track stacks up against industry standards and guides you in making necessary adjustments. Tools like Adaptr Audio's Metric

AB can facilitate easy A/B comparisons, allowing you to switch between your track and the reference seamlessly.

Testing playback in different environments is also essential. Take your master outside the studio and play it in various real-world settings. Listen in a car, where bass frequencies can become overwhelming, or in a living room, where midrange frequencies might dominate. Public spaces can also provide valuable insights, especially if there's background noise competing with your track. These tests help you identify and address any issues that only become apparent in specific environments.

When you encounter translation issues, there are several techniques that can help resolve them. Adjusting EQ is often the first step. If certain frequencies are too prominent or too subdued, make subtle EQ adjustments to balance them out. For instance, if the bass is overpowering on consumer speakers, a gentle cut in the low frequencies can help. Compression settings might also need tweaking. If the dynamic response feels off on certain systems, adjust the attack and release times to achieve a more natural sound. Finally, make subtle adjustments to levels and panning. Small changes can significantly impact how the mix translates across different systems, ensuring each element sits well in the overall mix.

Metering tools are invaluable in mastering. They provide visual aids that help you make informed decisions about levels, frequency content, and stereo imaging. Loudness meters, for instance, show the overall volume of your track in LUFS (Loudness Units Full Scale), ensuring that your master meets the loudness standards of streaming platforms. Spectrum analyzers display the frequency balance of your mix, helping you identify any imbalances that need addressing. Phase correlation meters show the phase relationship between the left and right channels, ensuring that your stereo imaging is accurate and that your track will sound good in mono as well.

Using these metering tools effectively can make a significant difference in the quality of your master. Loudness meters help you maintain consistent volume levels, avoiding the pitfalls of overly loud or too quiet tracks. Spectrum analyzers guide you in achieving a balanced frequency response, ensuring no particular frequency range dominates. Phase correlation meters ensure that your stereo imaging is precise, preventing phase cancellation issues when your track is played in mono.

Mastering is about more than just making your track loud. It's about ensuring it sounds good everywhere, from the best studio monitors to the simplest earbuds. By using a combination of listening tests, reference tracks, EQ adjustments, and metering tools, you can create a master that translates well across all systems. This process ensures that your music reaches its full potential, delivering a consistent and impactful listening experience regardless of the playback environment.

As you master these techniques, you'll find that your tracks sound better and hold up in any setting, providing a consistent and enjoyable listening experience for your audience. This holistic approach to mastering ties together all the skills and knowledge you've gained, preparing you for the next step in your audio production journey.

Chapter Ten

Troubleshooting Common Issues

We remember a session where everything seemed perfect until playback revealed a distorted mess. Our hearts sank. We had captured what we thought was a great performance, only to find it marred by unwanted noise and artifacts. This chapter is here to help you avoid those moments of frustration by understanding and addressing common causes of audio artifacts and distortion.

Fixing Audio Artifacts and Distortion

Unwanted audio artifacts and distortion can ruin an otherwise perfect recording. Understanding the common causes can help you avoid these pitfalls. One primary culprit is clipping, which occurs when input levels are set too high. This causes the audio signal to exceed the system's threshold, leading to a flattened, distorted waveform. Poor quality or faulty cables and connections can also introduce noise and distortion, as can software glitches and buffer underruns. These issues can arise from pushing your recording equipment beyond its limits or from environmental factors like radio frequency (RF) interference and electrical noise.

Preventing audio artifacts requires a proactive approach. Proper gain staging is crucial to avoid clipping. Set your input levels to peak in the green zone on your level meters, with occasional dips into the yellow. Red indicates clipping, which you want to avoid. Using high-quality, shielded cables can minimize noise and ensure a clean signal path.

Shielded cables protect against RF interference, which can introduce unwanted noise. Ensuring adequate buffer size in your DAW settings can prevent buffer underruns. A larger buffer size reduces the likelihood of glitches during recording and playback, though it may increase latency.

When audio artifacts and distortion do occur, several techniques can help clean up the recordings. De-clip plugins are designed to repair clipped audio by analyzing the surrounding audio and reconstructing the lost waveform. Tools like iZotope RX and CrumplePop ClipRemover are excellent for this purpose. Spectral repair tools allow you to visually identify and remove specific artifacts. These tools display the audio signal as a spectrogram, enabling you to pinpoint and address problem areas. Manual editing techniques, such as cutting out the distorted section and replacing it with a clean take or using crossfades, can also be effective for fixing minor issues.

Case Study: Repairing a Distorted Vocal Track

Consider the case of a distorted vocal track recorded during a live session. The clipping occurred because the input levels were set too high, causing the signal to exceed the threshold. Using a de-clip plugin, the engineer was able to analyze the clipped sections and reconstruct the waveform, significantly reducing the distortion. To further clean up the track, spectral repair tools were applied to remove any remaining artifacts. The result was a clear and professional-sounding vocal recording.

Another example involves using spectral repair on a guitar recording. The recording session was plagued by electrical noise due to poor-quality cables. The engineer used spectral repair tools to visually identify the noise frequencies and remove them without affecting the rest of the audio. The final result was a clean guitar track free of unwanted noise.

Understanding the common causes of audio artifacts and distortion, along with implementing preventive measures and using effective repair techniques, can significantly improve the quality of your recordings. By addressing these issues head-on, you can ensure that your audio projects sound professional and polished, no matter the circumstances.

Synchronization Problems and How to Solve Them

Synchronization is crucial in audio production. It ensures that all elements of a project align perfectly in time. Whether you're working on a multi-track recording, a live session, or a multimedia project, proper synchronization is key to maintaining coherence. Imagine recording multiple takes of a vocal performance. If those takes don't line up perfectly, you'll end up with timing issues that can ruin the recording. Synchronization also plays a vital role in multimedia projects where audio needs to match video. Misaligned audio and video can create a disjointed experience, making your production seem unprofessional.

Common causes of synchronization problems often involve latency in recording and playback. Latency is the delay between the input signal and its playback, and even a slight delay can throw off your entire project. Drift between digital and analog devices is another issue. Digital devices are precise, but analog devices can drift over time, causing misalignment. Inconsistent frame rates in video projects can also lead to synchronization challenges. If your audio and video run at different frame rates, they won't stay in sync, resulting in timing discrepancies that become more pronounced over time.

Resolving synchronization issues requires a combination of techniques and tools. Using timecode and sync clocks for precise alignment is one effective method. Timecode provides a reference that all devices can follow, ensuring they stay in sync. Sync clocks send a common timing signal to all connected devices, keeping everything locked together. Adjusting buffer settings in your DAW can help minimize latency. A smaller buffer size reduces latency, but be mindful that it may increase the load on your computer's CPU. Aligning audio manually within the DAW is another practical approach, especially when dealing with minor misalignments. Zoom in on the waveform and manually drag the audio to align it with other tracks.

Specific tools and techniques can assist with synchronization. When syncing audio with video, use frame rate matching to ensure both run at the same rate. This prevents timing issues that can arise from mismatched frame rates. Plugins like Auto-Align are invaluable for phase and timing correction. They analyze the timing and phase of multiple tracks and adjust them automatically, ensuring perfect alignment. A practical example is syncing a multi-camera shoot with audio. Each camera and audio recorder may have slight timing differences. By using timecode and sync clocks, you can ensure all devices stay in sync throughout the shoot. In post-production, align the audio and video manually within your editing software to fine-tune the synchronization.

Using timecode and sync clocks involves setting up each device to follow the same timecode source. For instance, in a studio setting, you might have your DAW, audio interface, and external hardware all synced to a master clock. This master clock sends a timing signal to each device, ensuring they stay in perfect sync. In a live recording scenario, you might use a timecode generator to embed timecode into the audio and video files. This allows you to align them precisely in post-production.

Adjusting buffer settings in your DAW can significantly reduce latency. A smaller buffer size means less delay between input and playback, but it also requires more processing power. Start with a medium buffer size and gradually reduce it while monitoring your system's performance. If your computer starts to struggle, increase the buffer size slightly. Finding the right balance between low latency and stable performance is key.

Manual alignment within the DAW involves zooming in on the waveform and aligning it visually. This is particularly useful for live recordings where slight timing discrepancies can occur. By manually adjusting the timing of each track, you can ensure they all line up perfectly. This method requires a keen eye and patience, but it can be incredibly effective for fine-tuning synchronization.

Using frame rate matching in video projects ensures that your audio and video remain in sync. Set your video editing software to match the frame rate of your audio recording. This prevents timing discrepancies when the audio and video run at different rates. If your video is recorded at 30 frames per second (fps), ensure your audio project is set to the same frame rate. This simple step can save you a lot of headaches in post-production.

Plugins like Auto-Align are designed to simplify the synchronization process. They work by analyzing the timing and phase of multiple tracks and making the necessary adjustments automatically. This is particularly useful in complex projects with multiple microphones capturing the same source. Auto-Align ensures all tracks are perfectly in sync, eliminating phase issues and timing discrepancies. Other plugins offer similar functionality, allowing you to focus on the creative aspects of your project rather than technical challenges.

In a practical scenario, consider a multi-camera shoot for a live concert. Each camera and audio recorder will have slight timing differences due to varying start times and potential drift. Using timecode, you can embed a reference signal into each recording. In post-production, these timecodes allow you to align each audio and video file precisely. Sync clocks can further ensure that all devices remain in perfect sync throughout the recording. In your video editing software, manually align the audio and video to fine-tune the synchronization, ensuring a seamless final product.

Understanding and addressing synchronization problems is crucial for maintaining the integrity of your audio projects. By implementing these techniques and utilizing the right tools, you can ensure that your projects remain coherent and professional, no matter the complexity.

Identifying and Resolving Phase Issues

One day while mixing a drum track, we noticed something off. The kick drum sounded weak, and the snare lacked its usual punch. It didn't take long to realize we was dealing with phase issues. Phase refers to the timing relationship between sound waves. When two or more audio signals are out of phase, they can either cancel each other out or reinforce each other, leading to phase cancellation or reinforcement. Phase cancellation can make your audio sound thin, hollow, or even cause certain frequencies to disappear. Conversely, phase reinforcement can lead to a boomy and uneven mix. Understanding how phase relationships work is crucial for any audio professional.

Phase issues often occur in scenarios where multiple microphones capture the same source. For instance, when miking a drum kit, the snare mic, overheads, and room mics can pick up the same snare hit at slightly different times. This timing difference can cause phase cancellation, making the snare sound weak. Another common scenario is mixing direct and ambient microphone signals. For example, when combining a DI signal of a guitar with a mic'd amp, the slight delay between the two signals can create phase issues. Even combining mono and stereo recordings can lead to phase problems, especially if the mono track is panned to one side in the stereo field.

Detecting phase issues requires a keen ear and the right tools. Phase correlation meters are invaluable for this purpose. These meters visually display the phase relationship between two audio signals. If the meter shows a positive correlation, your signals are in phase. A negative correlation indicates phase issues. Listening for comb filtering and hollow sounds is another practical method. Comb filtering occurs when two similar audio signals combine, causing a series of peaks and nulls in the frequency response. This results in a hollow, filtered sound. Comparing signals in mono can also help identify phase problems. When you switch to mono, phase cancellation becomes more apparent, making it easier to detect and address.

Fixing phase issues involves several techniques. Adjusting microphone placement is the first line of defense. Ensuring that microphones are equidistant from the sound source can minimize phase issues. For example, when miking a drum kit, make sure the overheads are the same distance from the snare. Using phase alignment plugins can also correct timing discrepancies. Plugins like Auto-Align analyze the phase relationship between tracks and make precise adjustments to align them. Inverting the phase on specific tracks is another useful technique. If two tracks are out of phase, inverting the phase on one track can bring them back into alignment. This is particularly effective for correcting phase issues between close and room mics.

Practical Example: Fixing Phase Issues in a Drum Recording

Consider a drum recording where the snare sounds weak and lacks impact. The phase issues likely stem from the overhead and snare mics picking up the snare hit at different times. Start by checking the phase correlation using a phase meter. If the meter shows a negative correlation, you have a phase problem. Next, try inverting the phase on the snare mic channel. This simple adjustment can often resolve phase issues instantly. If the problem persists, use a phase alignment plugin like Auto-Align. Insert the plugin on both the snare and overhead tracks, and let it analyze and correct the phase alignment. The result should be a snare that sounds punchy and well-defined, with no hollow or weak spots.

Understanding phase and knowing how to identify and resolve phase issues is vital for achieving a clear and powerful mix. Whether you're dealing with multiple microphones, direct and ambient signals, or mono and stereo recordings, mastering phase relationships can significantly improve your audio quality. As you refine your techniques and tools, you'll find that your mixes become more cohesive and impactful, bringing your audio projects to a professional standard.

As we wrap up this chapter on troubleshooting common issues, remember that every challenge is an opportunity to improve your skills and knowledge. From fixing audio artifacts and distortion to solving synchronization problems and resolving phase issues, each step brings you closer to mastering the nuances of audio production. Up next, we'll explore how to stay current with industry trends, ensuring that your skills and techniques remain sharp and relevant in a rapidly evolving field.

Chapter Eleven

Staying Current with Industry Trends

One day, while working in our home studio, we stumbled upon a new AI-driven mastering service called LANDR. We had heard about AI in various fields, but seeing it applied to audio production was a revelation. The idea that artificial intelligence could analyze and enhance our tracks, making them sound professional without the need for a high-end studio, was both thrilling and a bit intimidating. This chapter explores how emerging technologies like AI, VR, AR, blockchain, and cloud-based tools are transforming audio production, making it more accessible and innovative for everyone.

Emerging Technologies in Audio Production

Artificial intelligence (AI) is revolutionizing the landscape of music and sound creation. AI-driven mastering services, such as LANDR, have democratized the mastering process, making it accessible to producers of all levels. LANDR uses sophisticated algorithms to analyze your tracks and apply a customized mastering chain unique to each one. The service offers unlimited revisions, album mastering, volume matching, and optimized outputs for streaming. This means you can achieve professional-quality mastering without the need for expensive gear or specialized knowledge. The technology behind LANDR is trusted by Grammy winners and over five million musicians, highlighting its credibility and effectiveness in the industry.

Beyond mastering, AI is making waves in sound design and music composition. Machine learning algorithms are now capable of generating new sounds and even entire compositions. Tools like Samplab allow you to edit individual notes within a sample, offering unprecedented control over your music. This software can detect chords and separate stems and integrate seamlessly with popular DAWs, making your workflow more efficient. AI platforms like Suno enable effortless music creation by allowing users to generate complete tracks based on genre and inputted lyrics or themes. These innovations streamline the creative process, allowing you to focus more on your artistic vision and less on technical constraints.

Virtual reality (VR) and augmented reality (AR) are also reshaping the audio production landscape. Binaural recording techniques, which use two microphones to create a 3D stereo sound sensation, are becoming increasingly popular. This approach replicates the human ear's listening experience, capturing spatial qualities of sound that traditional recording methods miss. Binaural recordings are particularly effective in VR and AR environments, where immersive audio enhances the overall experience. For instance, in gaming, spatial audio tools create 360-degree soundscapes that make players feel like they are truly inside the game world. In live performances and installations, VR and AR can transform how audiences experience music, offering interactive and immersive experiences that were previously unimaginable.

Blockchain technology is another game-changer in the music industry, particularly in the realm of digital rights management and artist compensation. Traditional music rights management systems are often complex and inefficient, failing to ensure fair payments to artists. Blockchain offers a more transparent and secure solution by tracking music usage and ensuring prompt royalty distribution. Blockchain-based platforms simplify the licensing process with smart contracts, which automatically execute agreements when predefined conditions are met. This reduces disputes and builds trust among artists, producers, and distributors. A successful case study in this area is the implementation of blockchain by independent artists who have seen faster payments and greater control over their music.

Cloud-based audio production tools are enhancing remote collaboration and production. Platforms like Soundtrap and BandLab offer cloud DAWs that facilitate real-time collaboration, allowing multiple users to work on the same project simultaneously. These tools are particularly useful for remote teams or artists who collaborate across different locations. Cloud storage ensures that your projects are always backed up and accessible, reducing the risk of data loss. Additionally, these platforms provide a wealth of resources, such as royalty-free samples, effects, and mastering tools, all integrated into the cloud ecosystem. This makes it easier to produce high-quality music without needing extensive local storage or expensive software.

Incorporating these emerging technologies into your workflow can significantly enhance your production capabilities. AI tools can handle complex tasks like mastering and sound design, freeing you to focus on creativity. VR and AR technologies can create immersive audio experiences that captivate audiences. Blockchain can ensure fair compensation and transparent rights management, while cloud-based tools facilitate seamless collaboration and provide robust resources. Staying current with these trends keeps your skills relevant and opens up new possibilities for innovation and creativity in your audio projects.

Evolving Trends in Music Production

The music production landscape is constantly evolving, shaped by emerging technologies, cultural shifts, and the creative exploration of artists worldwide. Here are some of the enduring trends that continue to influence the world of music production:

Blending Genres and Creating Hybrid Sounds

One of the most significant ongoing trends in music production is blending genres to create new, hybrid sounds. Producers are increasingly experimenting with combining electronic beats with classical instruments, mixing hip-hop rhythms with jazz melodies, or integrating world music elements into mainstream pop. Technological advances, such as sophisticated digital audio workstations (DAWs) and versatile plugins, have made it easier to manipulate and merge sounds. This trend reflects a broader movement toward a more inclusive and diverse soundscape where traditional genre boundaries are continually blurred, allowing for innovative and unique creations.

The Resurgence of Analog and Vintage Sounds

Despite the digital revolution, there's a growing appreciation for the warmth and character of analog gear, such as synthesizers, drum machines, and tape recorders. Many producers are rediscovering analog equipment's tactile experience and organic sounds, finding that these tools offer a unique layer of creativity often missing in digital setups. The imperfections, quirks, and depth that analog gear brings to music can provide a sense of authenticity that stands out in today's digital landscape. This trend isn't just about nostalgia but the creative possibilities of blending the old with the new.

The Impact of Social Media and Short-Form Content

Social media platforms like TikTok, Instagram, and YouTube have profoundly impacted music production trends. These platforms have democratized music discovery, enabling artists to reach global audiences instantly. Viral production techniques inspired by social media trends are now commonplace. Producers often craft songs with catchy hooks, short structures, and looping sections to maximize shareability and listener engagement. The format of short-form content has influenced song structure, encouraging quick intros and memorable choruses to capture attention within seconds. This trend continues to shape how music is produced, marketed, and consumed.

The Rise of Experimental and Minimalist Production Techniques

Producers are increasingly embracing experimental approaches to sound design and production. This can range from creating soundscapes using unconventional instruments and field recordings to minimalistic setups focusing on the purity of a few well-chosen sounds rather than complex arrangements. The trend toward minimalism is also evident in the growing interest in lo-fi and ambient music, where simplicity and emotional resonance precede highly polished production. These evolving styles reflect a desire to create more intimate and reflective music experiences.

Sustainability and Eco-Friendly Production Practices

As environmental awareness grows, artists and producers adopt sustainable practices in their studios and production processes. This includes using energy-efficient equipment, reducing waste, and choosing eco-friendly materials for vinyl pressing and packaging. Some recording studios are now powered entirely by renewable energy, such as solar, and incorporate sustainable materials for soundproofing and acoustic treatment. This shift toward sustainability will continue as the industry and artists increasingly recognize their environmental impact.

Virtual and Immersive Experiences

Live streaming and virtual performances have evolved beyond a temporary solution and are now integral to the music industry. Platforms like Twitch, YouTube Live, and specialized virtual concert platforms offer robust tools for artists to connect with audiences in real-time. These platforms have introduced monetization strategies, such as subscriptions, virtual merchandise, and interactive fan experiences, making them valuable for artists seeking new revenue streams. The growing field of virtual and augmented reality is pushing this trend further, creating immersive concert experiences that replicate or even enhance the feel of live shows.

By staying attuned to these ongoing trends, music producers can find endless opportunities for innovation and creativity. From blending genres and embracing the warmth of analog sounds to leveraging the power of social media and sustainability, the evolving landscape of music production offers a dynamic space for artists to experiment, grow, and connect with audiences worldwide.

Staying Updated with Software and Plug-Ins

Keeping up with new software releases is crucial for staying ahead in audio production. One effective strategy is to follow industry news and forums. Websites like Gearspace and Reddit's r/audioengineering are treasure troves of information where professionals and enthusiasts discuss the latest updates and share their experiences. Subscribing to newsletters from software developers is another great way to stay informed. Companies like Ableton, Native Instruments, and Waves often send out emails announcing new features, updates, and special offers. Participating in beta testing programs can also give you early access to upcoming releases. Not only does this allow you to try new features before they hit the market, but it also gives you a chance to provide feedback and help shape the development of the software.

Regularly updating your plugins is just as important. Keeping plugins up-to-date ensures they run smoothly with the latest DAW versions and operating systems. Updates often include new features and bug fixes that can enhance performance and security. For instance, a new update might introduce a more efficient algorithm that reduces CPU load, allowing you to run more plugins simultaneously. Using plugin managers can make this process easier. Tools like Native Access and Waves Central streamline the update process, ensuring all your plugins are current with just a few clicks.

In the past year, several innovative plugins have made waves in the industry. New virtual instruments and sample libraries have expanded the creative possibilities for producers. For example, Spitfire Audio's "Abbey Road One: Orchestral Foundations" offers stunning orchestral sounds recorded at the legendary Abbey Road Studios. Cutting-edge effects plugins like FabFilter Pro-Q 3, a dynamic EQ that allows for precise frequency adjustments, are also game-changers. Innovative mixing and mastering tools, such as iZotope Ozone 9, combine multiple modules to provide an all-in-one solution for finalizing your tracks. These plugins enhance the quality of your productions and streamline your workflow, saving you time and effort.

Evaluating and choosing new plugins can be overwhelming, given the vast options available. Start by reading reviews and watching demo videos. Websites like Sound on Sound and YouTube channels like Produce Like a Pro offer in-depth reviews and demonstrations. Trying free trials and demo versions is another effective way to assess a plugin's value. Most developers offer trial periods, allowing you to test the plugin in your projects before committing to a purchase. Consider how the plugin will integrate into your workflow. Check its compatibility with your DAW and other plugins, and consider its system requirements to ensure it runs smoothly on your setup.

Investing in the right plugins can significantly elevate your productions. Whether you're looking for new sounds, creative effects, or powerful mixing tools, staying updated with the latest software ensures you have the best tools at your disposal. This enhances the quality of your work and keeps you competitive in a rapidly evolving industry.

Staying current with software and plugins is a continuous process that requires active engagement with the audio production community. You can stay ahead of the curve by following industry news, participating in beta testing, and regularly updating your tools. Evaluating new plugins through reviews, demos, and trials ensures you make informed decisions that enhance your workflow and creative output.

As we wrap up this chapter, remember that the tools you use are just one part of the equation. Your skills, creativity, and dedication are what truly make your productions shine. In the next chapter, we'll explore resourceful budgeting and DIY solutions, helping you achieve professional results without breaking the bank.

Chapter Twelve

Resourceful Budgeting and DIY Solutions

We remember the exhilaration of unboxing our first piece of audio gear. It was a budget microphone we had saved up for months. we knew it wasn't top-of-the-line, but we were determined to make it work. That experience taught us the value of choosing the right budget gear. You don't need the most expensive equipment to create high-quality audio. With the right choices and a bit of creativity, you can achieve professional results without breaking the bank.

Budget-Friendly Alternatives to High-End Gear

Choosing the right budget gear is essential for anyone looking to produce high-quality audio without spending a fortune. Research and reviews are your best friends in this endeavor. Before making any purchase, take the time to read reviews and watch video demonstrations. Websites like Sound on Sound and forums like Gearspace offer valuable insights from professionals and enthusiasts. These resources can help you identify which budget gear performs well and which options to avoid.

One of the best aspects of budget gear is its upgrade potential. Many entry-level pieces of equipment can be enhanced over time. For example, you might start with a basic audio interface and later add external preamps or better microphones as your budget allows. This incremental approach ensures you're always improving your setup without needing a massive upfront investment.

For those starting out, several budget-friendly alternatives can provide excellent results. The Focusrite Scarlett series, particularly the Scarlett 2i2, is a fantastic choice for an audio interface. It offers 24-bit/192 kHz resolution and features like Auto Gain and Clip Safe, which help prevent distortion. Another excellent option is the Behringer UMC series, known for its solid build quality and reliable performance. If you're on an even tighter budget, the M-Audio M-Track Solo is a great pick, offering essential features at a very affordable price.

When it comes to microphones, the Audio-Technica AT2020 and Shure SM57 are standout choices. The AT2020 is a versatile condenser mic that excels at capturing vocals and acoustic instruments with clarity. The Shure SM57, on the other hand, is a dynamic mic renowned for its ruggedness and ability to handle high sound pressure levels, making it perfect for recording electric guitars and drums.

For studio monitors, the JBL 305P MkII and KRK Rokit 5 G4 provide excellent value. The JBL 305P MkII offers a balanced frequency response and wide sweet spot, making it ideal for accurate mixing. The KRK Rokit 5 G4 features a built-in EQ with room tuning options, allowing you to tailor the sound to your specific environment.

Used and refurbished gear can also be a cost-effective solution. Websites like Reverb and eBay offer a wide range of pre-owned equipment. When shopping for used gear, always check the seller's ratings and read any reviews or comments from previous buyers. It's essential to verify the condition and functionality of the equipment before finalizing your purchase. Look for signs of wear and tear, and ask the seller for a demo video or sound samples if possible.

Proper setup and calibration are crucial to making the most of your budget gear. Ensure your audio interface is correctly configured in your DAW and your microphones are positioned optimally for the best sound capture. Using free or affordable software plugins can significantly enhance your recordings. Plugins like TDR Nova for EQ and the Valhalla Supermassive for reverb provide professional-quality effects without the hefty price tag.

Regular maintenance and care can extend the lifespan of your gear. Clean your microphones regularly and store them in protective cases to prevent dust and damage. Keep your cables organized and free from kinks to avoid signal degradation. Periodically check for software updates for your audio interface and DAW to ensure optimal performance and compatibility.

Quick Checklist for Optimizing Budget Gear:

- Research and Reviews: Utilize resources like Sound on Sound and Gearspace.

- Upgrade Over Time: Start with essential gear and add enhancements as your budget allows.

- Audio Interfaces: Consider Focusrite Scarlett 2i2, Behringer UMC series, or M-Audio M-Track Solo.

- Microphones: Choose versatile options like Audio-Technica AT2020 and Shure SM57.

- Studio Monitors: Opt for JBL 305P MkII or KRK Rokit 5 G4.

- Used Gear: Shop on Reverb and eBay, verify condition, and check seller ratings.

- Setup and Calibration: Ensure proper configuration and microphone placement.

- Software Plugins: Use free or affordable options like TDR Nova and Valhalla Supermassive.

- Maintenance: Clean and store gear properly, organize cables, and update software regularly.

By carefully selecting and maintaining your budget gear, you can achieve high-quality audio production without needing top-of-the-line equipment. This approach lets you focus on honing your skills and creativity, knowing your gear won't hold you back.

DIY Acoustic Panels and Bass Traps

Acoustic treatment can significantly improve the sound quality of your home studio. Proper treatment reduces reflections and standing waves, enhancing the clarity and accuracy of your recordings and mixes. Reflections occur when sound waves bounce off hard surfaces like walls, ceilings, and floors. These reflections can create echoes and reverb, muddying the sound and making it difficult to achieve a clean recording. Standing waves, on the other hand, happen when sound waves of certain frequencies resonate in the room, causing peaks and nulls in the frequency response. These issues can be particularly problematic in small or irregularly shaped rooms.

Building your own acoustic panels is a cost-effective way to tackle these problems. You'll need a few materials: Rockwool or fiberglass insulation, wooden frames, and fabric. The tools required include a saw, staple gun, and measuring tape. Start by cutting the wooden boards to the desired size. For a standard panel, you'll need two pieces of 48" x 1"x4" and two pieces of 23" x 1"x4". Next, glue and fasten the boards together to form a rectangular frame. Use a brad nailer or small screws for added strength. Once the frame is assembled, attach screen door material to one side using a staple gun. This material will hold the insulation in place. Insert the insulation into the frame, making sure it fits snugly. Cover the other side with more screen material, then stretch fabric over the front and secure it with staples. Trim any excess fabric, and your acoustic panel is ready.

Bass traps are another crucial element of acoustic treatment, specifically designed to control low-frequency issues. These traps are typically placed in corners where bass frequencies tend to build up. To create a bass trap, you'll need dense insulation, plywood, and fabric. Start by cutting the plywood into triangular pieces that will fit in the corners of your room. Build a frame using these pieces and fill it with dense insulation. Cover the frame with fabric, securing it with staples. The thickness and density of the insulation help absorb low frequencies, reducing the impact of standing waves and creating a more balanced sound.

Placement is key for both acoustic panels and bass traps. Acoustic panels should be placed at first reflection points, which are the spots where sound first bounces off a surface before reaching your ears. You can find these points by using a mirror: have someone move the mirror along the walls while you sit at your mixing position. Where you see the reflection of your speakers in the mirror is where you should place your panels. Bass traps should be placed in the corners of the room, as this is where low frequencies accumulate. For maximum effectiveness, consider placing traps in all four corners, including the ceiling corners if possible.

Real-world examples can illustrate the impact of DIY acoustic treatments. Take, for instance, a small bedroom studio that was transformed using homemade panels and traps. Before treatment, the room suffered from significant reflections and standing waves, making it difficult to achieve clean recordings. After installing DIY acoustic panels at the first reflection points and bass traps in the corners, the difference was night and day. The room became much more controlled, and the recordings were clearer and more accurate.

Case studies further highlight the benefits of DIY acoustic treatments. One user transformed a small, square room into a functional recording space by building and installing their own panels and traps. They used affordable materials like Rockwool insulation and fabric from a local craft store. By following the steps outlined above, they managed to create a professional-sounding environment on a tight budget. The result was a significant improvement in the quality of their recordings and mixes, demonstrating that you don't need expensive gear to achieve great sound.

Testimonials from others who have implemented DIY solutions also speak volumes. Many have reported substantial improvements in their studio environments, citing clearer sound, better mixes, and more enjoyable recording sessions. These success stories underscore the value of taking the time to build and install your own acoustic treatments. Not only do you save money, but you also gain a deeper understanding of how sound behaves in your space.

Acoustic treatment is a critical aspect of creating a professional-quality home studio. By building your own panels and bass traps, you can effectively manage reflections and standing waves, leading to clearer, more accurate recordings and mixes. With a bit of effort and some affordable materials, you can transform your recording space and elevate the quality of your audio production.

12.3 Maximizing Your Setup with Limited Resources

When working with limited resources, maximizing your setup is crucial to achieving professional results. Begin by prioritizing essential gear and upgrades. Focus on the core components of your setup that will have the most significant impact on your sound, such as your audio interface, microphones, and monitors. Once you have a solid foundation, you can gradually add enhancements like better preamps or additional plugins. This approach ensures that your upgrades are strategic and contribute meaningfully to your overall sound quality.

Using your existing equipment creatively can also make a significant difference. For instance, a single microphone can serve multiple purposes with the right techniques. You can record vocals, instruments, and even use it as an overhead for drums. Experiment with different placements and settings to discover new ways to utilize your gear. Additionally, repurposing items you already have can save money. For example, an old bookshelf can become a makeshift diffuser to help control reflections in your room.

Efficient workflow practices are another way to make the most of your setup. Establish a consistent routine for setting up and breaking down your equipment. This saves time and ensures that your gear is always ready for use. Organize your cables and accessories so everything is easy to find and access. Creating a template for your DAW sessions can also streamline your workflow. Preload commonly used tracks, plugins, and settings so you can jump straight into creating without wasting time on setup.

Optimizing your workspace is essential, especially when dealing with limited space. Arrange your furniture and equipment to facilitate an efficient workflow. Place your desk and monitors in the center of the room, with your speakers forming an equilateral triangle with your listening position. Use vertical space for storage by installing shelves or wall-mounted racks. This keeps your workspace tidy and frees up floor space for movement. Consider creating a multifunctional space that can serve various purposes, such as recording, mixing, and even relaxation. Foldable furniture and mobile carts can help you quickly reconfigure the room as needed.

Free and affordable software alternatives can significantly enhance your setup without breaking the bank. Free Digital Audio Workstations (DAWs) like Audacity and Reaper offer robust features for recording, editing, and mixing. Audacity is straightforward and user-friendly, making it ideal for beginners. Reaper, on the other hand, offers extensive customization and supports all major plugin formats, making it suitable for more advanced users. Free plugins like TDR Nova, a dynamic equalizer, and Valhalla Supermassive, a versatile reverb, provide professional-quality effects without the cost. Affordable virtual instruments like Native Instruments Komplete Start offer a range of sounds and instruments to expand your creative possibilities. Open-source and community-supported projects can also provide valuable resources and tools. Platforms like GitHub host a variety of free plugins and software developed by the audio community.

Practical examples and success stories illustrate how others have maximized their setups with limited resources. One notable case study involves an independent musician who produced a professional album using minimal gear. They recorded vocals with a single-budget microphone and used a basic audio interface. By creatively layering tracks and using free plugins, they achieved a rich and polished sound. Another example is a content creator who optimized their home studio for podcasting. They used affordable acoustic panels to treat their room and free software like Audacity for recording and editing. Their efficient workflow allowed them to produce high-quality episodes consistently.

Testimonials from home studio users who have successfully optimized their setups further demonstrate the potential of limited resources. Many have reported significant improvements in their production quality and efficiency by implementing the strategies discussed. These success stories underscore the importance of creativity, organization, and resourcefulness in audio production.

Maximizing your setup with limited resources involves prioritizing essential gear, using existing equipment creatively, and optimizing your workspace. Free and affordable software alternatives can enhance your production capabilities, while practical examples and success stories illustrate the potential of these strategies. With a bit of ingenuity and careful planning, you can achieve professional-quality audio production without needing a high-end studio. Next, we'll explore the importance of developing critical listening skills and how to enhance your ability to produce high-quality audio.

Chapter Thirteen

Technical Writing for Audio Professionals

Imagine this: you've just wrapped up a recording session with a band that nailed every take. The energy was electric, and you captured some truly magical moments. A week later, you're back in the studio for mixing, and you can't remember which mic you used for the lead vocals or the exact settings on your preamp. The frustration sets in, and you realize you didn't document the session details. This scenario underscores the critical importance of meticulous recording session documentation.

Documenting Your Recording Sessions

Keeping accurate records during your recording sessions is crucial for several reasons. First, it ensures consistency across sessions. When you document every detail, you can easily replicate the setup for future sessions, maintaining a consistent sound. This is especially important when working on albums or projects that span multiple sessions. Consistency in your recordings can make the mixing and mastering process much smoother, as you won't need to compensate for variations in sound.

Detailed documentation also facilitates collaboration with other audio professionals. When you share your session notes with a mixing engineer, they'll have a clear understanding of the recording setup, which can inform their mixing decisions. Similarly, if you're collaborating with other producers or musicians, detailed notes can help everyone stay on the same page, ensuring a cohesive final product. Providing a reference for mixing and mastering stages is another significant benefit. By documenting settings such as microphone positions, preamp settings, and EQ adjustments, you provide a roadmap for the mixing and mastering engineers. They can use this information to make informed decisions, leading to a polished and professional final product.

Legal and copyright considerations are also important. Detailed documentation can serve as proof of your work, protecting your intellectual property and ensuring you receive proper credit. In disputes over authorship or contribution, well-documented session notes can be invaluable.

To help you get started, here's a structured template for recording session logs. Begin with the date and location of the session. This provides context and helps you track the progress of your project. Next, list the personnel involved. Include everyone from the artists to the engineers, as this can be useful for credits and future reference. Document the equipment and settings used. Note the types of microphones, their positions, and any specific settings like pads or filters. Include details about the preamps, compressors, and other outboard gear used. This level of detail ensures that you can replicate the setup if needed.

Best practices for taking session notes can make the process more efficient and effective. Using shorthand and abbreviations can save time while still capturing essential information. For example, you might use "LDC" for large-diaphragm condenser or "HPF" for high-pass filter. Noting any technical issues encountered and their solutions is crucial. If you experience a problem with a particular piece of gear, document it and the steps you took to resolve it. This can save time in future sessions and help you troubleshoot more effectively.

Documenting creative decisions and their rationale is equally important. If you decide to use a particular microphone for its unique character or choose a specific EQ setting to enhance a vocal, note these decisions. This helps you remember your creative choices and provides valuable insight for collaborators who may work on the project later.

To illustrate these practices, let's look at a practical example of a detailed vocal recording session log. Suppose you're recording a lead vocal for a pop track. Your log might include the date and location, such as "March 15, 2023, Home Studio." List the personnel involved: "Vocalist: Jane Doe, Engineer: John Smith." Document the equipment and settings: "Microphone: Neumann U87, positioned 6 inches from the vocalist, slightly off-axis; Preamp: SSL XLogic, gain set to 30 dB, with HPF engaged at 80 Hz." Note any technical issues: "Initial take had sibilance issues, resolved by adjusting mic position and using a de-esser plugin." Document creative decisions: "Choose U87 for its warm, detailed sound, which complements the bright arrangement."

For a multi-day recording project, your template might include additional sections for each day's activities, equipment changes, and any adjustments made. This comprehensive approach ensures that no detail is overlooked. For example, you might note, "Day 1: Recorded drums with Shure SM57 on snare, AKG D112 on kick, and Rode NT5 as overheads. Day 2: Recorded guitars with Shure SM57 and Royer R-121, adjusted amp settings for a brighter tone."

Including troubleshooting notes during a session can also be beneficial. For instance, if you encounter a grounding issue causing hum in your recordings, document the problem and the solution: "Encountered hum due to grounding issue, resolved by using a ground lift on DI box."

By implementing these practices, you'll create a robust documentation system that enhances your workflow, facilitates collaboration, and ensures the highest quality in your audio productions.

Writing Clear and Concise Technical Reports

Technical reports are an integral part of any audio production workflow. They provide a clear summary of technical processes and outcomes, which is crucial for effective communication among team members and stakeholders. When you're working on a project, everyone involved needs to understand what was done, how it was done, and what the results were. This transparency ensures that all team members are on the same page. Additionally, technical reports serve as valuable references for future projects or troubleshooting. By documenting your processes and outcomes, you create a resource that you or others can consult if similar issues arise in the future. This can save time and effort, making your workflow more efficient.

To write clear and concise technical reports, start by using plain language and avoiding jargon. While technical terms are often necessary, overloading your report with jargon can make it difficult to read and understand. Aim to explain concepts in simple terms. For instance, instead of saying "utilize the parametric equalizer to attenuate frequencies," you can say "use the EQ to reduce certain frequencies." Organize your information logically with headings and subheadings. This structure makes it easier for readers to navigate your report and find the information they need. Including visuals such as charts and diagrams can also enhance clarity. A well-placed graph can illustrate a point more effectively than a paragraph of text. For example, showing frequency response curves can help readers understand the impact of your EQ settings.

A well-structured technical report typically includes several key components. The introduction sets the stage by explaining the purpose and scope of the report. It should give readers an overview of what to expect and why the report is important. The methodology section provides a detailed description of the processes and techniques used. This section should be thorough enough that someone else could replicate your work based on your description. Include specific settings, equipment used, and any particular challenges you encountered. The results section is where you summarize your findings and outcomes. This is the heart of your report, where you present the data and observations that resulted from your work. Finally, the conclusion interprets the results and offers recommendations. This is your opportunity to explain what the results mean and suggest next steps or improvements.

For instance, imagine you've completed a complex mixing project. Your technical report might begin with an introduction explaining the project's goals: "This report details the mixing process for Artist X's latest single, aiming to achieve a clear and balanced final mix." The methodology section would describe your approach: "We used a combination of digital and analog gear, starting with a basic EQ to clean up the tracks, followed by compression to control dynamics. Specific settings included a 3 dB cut at 200 Hz on the kick drum to reduce muddiness and a 2:1 compression ratio on the vocals for consistency." The results section would present your findings: "After applying EQ and compression, the mix achieved a more balanced sound. The kick drum sat well in the mix, and the vocals were clear and present." The conclusion might offer recommendations: "For future projects, consider using a multiband compressor on the bass to achieve even better control over dynamics."

Similarly, if you're writing a troubleshooting report on equipment issues, the introduction would outline the problem: "This report addresses the persistent grounding issue encountered during our recent recording sessions." The methodology would detail your troubleshooting steps: "We inspected all cables and connections, used a ground lift on the DI box, and replaced faulty cables." The results would summarize the outcomes: "Implementing these measures eliminated the hum, resulting in clean recordings." The conclusion might suggest preventive measures: "Regularly inspect cables and connections to prevent similar issues in the future."

Here's a practical example of a report summarizing the results of an acoustic treatment project. The introduction might state: "This report documents the acoustic treatment applied to Studio A to improve sound quality." The methodology would describe the treatment process: "We installed six DIY acoustic panels on the walls and two bass traps in the corners. Measurements were taken before and after the installation using an SPL meter." The results would present the data: "Post-treatment measurements showed a significant reduction in early reflections and a smoother frequency response, particularly in the low end." The conclusion would interpret these findings: "The acoustic treatment effectively reduced problematic reflections and improved overall sound quality. Additional bass traps would further enhance low-frequency response."

By following these guidelines and using structured templates, you can create clear and concise technical reports that are easy to understand and highly informative. These reports will improve communication and collaboration and serve as valuable references for future projects.

Creating Effective Project Documentation

Imagine finalizing the mix for an album only to realize you need to retrace your steps to adjust a minor detail. Without comprehensive project documentation, you'd be navigating blind. Detailed project documentation is essential for ensuring continuity and consistency across different phases of a project. It helps maintain a coherent vision from pre-production to post-production, saving time and preventing errors. Consistency in documentation also facilitates collaboration and communication among team members. When everyone has access to the same information, miscommunications are minimized, and the workflow becomes smoother. This is crucial in collaborative environments where multiple people might be working on different aspects of a project at the same time or even at different times. Additionally, comprehensive documentation provides a valuable reference for future projects and revisions. Whether you need to recreate a setup or troubleshoot a recurring issue, detailed records serve as a reliable resource.

Effective project documentation should include several key components. First, a project overview and objectives set the stage by outlining the goals and scope of the project. This section helps keep the team aligned with the project's vision and ensures everyone is working towards the same goals. Next, a detailed timeline and milestones provide a roadmap for the project. This section should include key dates and deadlines, ensuring the project stays on track. Milestones can help break down the project into manageable phases, making it easier to monitor progress. An equipment list and technical specifications are essential for maintaining consistency in sound and quality. This section should detail all the equipment used, including microphones, preamps, interfaces, and any other gear. Technical specifications, such as sample rates and bit depths, should also be documented to ensure uniformity across sessions. Session logs and technical reports provide a detailed account of each recording session. These logs should include information about microphone placements, settings, and any issues encountered. Technical reports can summarize the processes and outcomes of each session, providing a clear picture of the project's progress.

Maintaining and organizing project documentation can be streamlined with the use of digital tools and software. Programs like Google Drive, Dropbox, or dedicated project management software such as Asana or Trello can help keep all documents in one place. These tools offer collaboration features, making it easy for team members to access and update documentation in real-time. Creating a consistent naming and filing system is also crucial. Use clear and descriptive filenames that include dates and key details. For example, "Vocal_Session_2023-04-01_U87_Settings.pdf" is more informative than "Session1.pdf." Organize files into folders based on the project's phases, such as pre-production, recording, and post-production. Regularly updating documentation to reflect changes and progress ensures the information remains accurate and useful. Schedule regular check-ins to review and update documents, especially after significant sessions or milestones.

To illustrate these practices, let's look at a practical example of comprehensive project documentation for an album production. Start with a project overview and objectives: "This project aims to produce a 10-track album for Artist Y, blending indie rock and electronic elements. The goal is to achieve a polished, radio-ready sound by the end of the year." Next, include a detailed timeline and milestones: "Pre-production (Jan-Feb), Recording (Mar-Jun), Mixing (Jul-Aug), Mastering (Sep), Release (Oct)." An equipment list and technical specifications should follow: "Microphones: Neumann U87, Shure SM7B; Preamps: API 512c, Universal Audio 6176; Interfaces: Focusrite Scarlett 18i20; Sample Rate: 48 kHz; Bit Depth: 24-bit." Session logs and technical reports can provide a detailed account of each session: "April 1, 2023: Recorded lead vocals for Track 3 using Neumann U87, positioned 6 inches from the vocalist, slightly off-axis. Preamp: Universal

Audio 6176, gain set to 35 dB. Encountered sibilance issues, resolved by repositioning the mic and using a de-esser plugin."

By implementing these practices and using structured templates, you can create a robust documentation system that enhances your workflow, facilitates collaboration, and ensures the highest quality in your audio productions. Effective project documentation is not just about keeping records—it's about creating a seamless process supporting audio production's creative and technical aspects.

As we move forward, we'll delve into practical exercises and real-world projects that will help you apply the concepts and techniques discussed in this book. These exercises are designed to reinforce your learning and provide hands-on experience in various aspects of audio production.

Chapter Fourteen

Practical Exercises and Real-World Projects

We remember the thrill of working on our first full song mixdown. The room was filled with the hum of gear, and our screen was brimming with tracks waiting to be shaped into a cohesive whole. The process was daunting yet exhilarating. Each step, from importing tracks to applying the final touches, was a journey in itself. This chapter is designed to guide you through that process, making it accessible and practical for your home studio setup.

Completing a Full Song Mixdown

Mixing a song from start to finish involves several key steps. The first step is importing and organizing your tracks. Start by loading all your audio files into your DAW. Label each track clearly—vocals, guitars, drums, bass, and any other elements you have. This organizational step is crucial. It sets the stage for a smooth workflow, allowing you to focus on creative decisions rather than searching for files. Group similar tracks together, like all drum elements or backing vocals, and use color-coding to visually differentiate them.

Next, set your initial levels and pans. Begin by zeroing out all your faders. Play through the track and start adjusting the levels of each element. Your goal is to create a rough balance. Listen critically and make sure no single element overpowers the others. Once the levels are set, move on to panning. Place elements in the stereo field to create width and separation. For instance, you might pan rhythm guitars left and right while keeping the lead vocal centered. This spatial arrangement helps each element find its place in the mix.

Applying EQ and compression comes next. EQ helps carve out space for each instrument. Begin by high-passing elements like vocals and guitars to remove unnecessary low frequencies. Use EQ to reduce muddiness and enhance clarity. For instance, cutting around 300 Hz can help clean up a vocal, while a boost around 2-4 kHz can add presence. Compression, on the other hand, controls dynamics. Apply gentle compression to vocals to even out the performance. For drums, use parallel compression to add punch without sacrificing dynamics.

Now, let's dive into a step-by-step guide for a mixdown project. Imagine you have a multi-track session of a rock band. Start by balancing levels and panning for clarity and separation. Set the kick and bass levels first, as they form the foundation of your mix. Gradually bring in the snare, toms, and cymbals, ensuring each element is audible and balanced. Pan the overheads and toms to create a wide stereo image. Next, add guitars, panning them left and right for width. Bring in the vocals last, making sure they sit comfortably above the mix without overpowering it.

Use EQ to carve out space for each instrument. For instance, if the guitars are clashing with the vocals, cut a small range around 2-3 kHz in the guitar tracks to make room for the vocals. Similarly, if the bass and kick are fighting for space, carve out a small notch in the bass around 60-80 Hz to let the kick punch through. Compression helps control dynamics. Apply it to the drum bus to glue the kit together. Use a slower attack to let the transients through and a fast release to maintain energy. For vocals, use a medium attack and release to smooth out the performance without making it sound squashed.

Add reverb and delay for depth and space. A short plate reverb on the snare can add brightness and character, while a longer hall reverb on the vocals can create an atmospheric effect. Use delay to add a sense of space. For instance, a slapback delay on the guitars can add depth without muddying the mix. Experiment with different reverb and delay settings to find what works best for your track.

Enhance your mix further with advanced techniques. Automation is a powerful tool for adding dynamic changes. Automate volume levels to emphasize certain parts of the song, like a vocal lift in the chorus or a subtle drop during a bridge. Use mid/side processing to enhance the stereo image. This technique allows you to process the mid and side signals separately, giving you more control over the stereo width. Add subtle effects for ear candy. For instance, use a bitcrusher on a background vocal for a unique texture or an auto-panner on a synth pad to create movement.

By following these steps and applying these techniques, you'll be able to create a professional-sounding mix right from your home studio.

Designing Soundscapes for Multimedia

Soundscapes play a crucial role in multimedia, whether it's in film, games, or other media formats. They create immersive environments that draw the audience into the narrative, enhancing the overall experience. A well-designed soundscape can transport viewers to a different world, making scenes more believable and engaging. For instance, the rustling leaves and distant bird calls in a forest scene can evoke a sense of tranquility, while the echoing footsteps in an empty hallway can build tension. By carefully crafting these auditory elements, you can support the visual and narrative components, making the audience feel like they are part of the story.

Creating a soundscape begins with analyzing the visual and narrative elements of your project. Watch the scene or play through the game level to understand its mood, setting, and key moments. Identify the sounds that are crucial for building this world. For a forest scene, this might include wind, rustling leaves, bird songs, and distant water streams. For a bustling cityscape, you might need traffic noise, chatter, footsteps, and distant sirens. Each sound should contribute to the atmosphere and support the narrative. Record or source these effects, making sure they are high-quality and appropriate for the context. You can use field recordings or find suitable sounds in sound libraries.

Layering and blending sounds is where the magic happens. Start by laying down a base layer of ambient sounds that set the scene. For a forest, this could be the gentle rustling of leaves and distant bird calls. Add more specific sounds on top, such as a nearby stream or footsteps on a path. Adjust the volume and EQ of each layer to ensure they blend seamlessly without overpowering each other. Spatial audio techniques can enhance realism. Pan sounds to different positions in the stereo field to create a sense of space. For instance, a bird call might pan from left to right, mimicking its movement across the scene. Use reverb and delay to place sounds within the environment, making them feel like they belong there.

Software tools are your best friends in this process. Digital Audio Workstations (DAWs) like Ableton Live or Logic Pro offer extensive capabilities for sound design.

Specialized software like Wwise or FMOD is particularly useful for game sound design, allowing you to implement interactive audio that reacts to player actions. Apply effects and processing to enhance realism. For instance, adjusting the reverb settings can make a forest sound spacious and open, while a city street might benefit from shorter, more reflective reverb settings. Use EQ to carve out unnecessary frequencies, ensuring each sound occupies its own space in the mix.

By following these steps and utilizing the tools and assets provided, you can create immersive and emotionally impactful soundscapes that enhance the overall experience of your multimedia projects.

Recording and Mixing a Live Performance

Recording a live performance presents a unique set of challenges. The first hurdle is dealing with ambient noise and bleed. In a live setting, you can't control the environment as you would in a studio. Audience chatter, venue acoustics, and stage noise all contribute to the ambient soundscape. This makes isolating individual instruments tricky. Microphone bleed—where mics pick up sounds from other sources—is another issue. A vocal mic might capture drum hits, or a guitar amp might bleed into the drum overheads. These factors can muddy the mix and require careful attention during recording and mixing.

Managing dynamic range and levels in a live setting is another significant challenge. Live performances are inherently dynamic, with sudden peaks and troughs in volume. Instruments might be played more aggressively, and vocalists might move closer or farther from the mic. Ensuring consistent levels without clipping requires vigilant monitoring and quick adjustments. Using compressors and limiters can help control these dynamics, but setting them correctly is crucial to avoid squashing the natural energy of the performance.

Proper mic placement and signal flow are essential. Start by setting up microphones and DI boxes. Use directional mics to minimize bleed and position them carefully to capture the best sound from each instrument. For instance, place mics close to the speaker cones of guitar amps and use shock mounts to reduce vibrations. DI boxes are useful for capturing clean signals from instruments like bass guitars and keyboards. Configure the recording setup by routing all mics and DI signals to a multi-channel interface. Ensure your signal flow is clean and free from hums and buzzes by checking cables and connections.

Monitoring and adjusting levels during the performance is critical. Use a mixing console or digital mixer to keep an eye on input levels. Aim for levels that peak around -6 to -12 dB to leave headroom and avoid clipping. Use headphones to monitor individual channels and make real-time adjustments as needed. Capturing audience and ambient sounds adds realism to your recording. Place a couple of mics facing the audience to capture their reactions and the overall room ambiance. These tracks can be mixed in later to give the recording a live feel.

Mixing live recordings requires techniques that differ from studio mixing. Start by balancing live tracks and reducing bleed. Use gating to minimize unwanted sounds and carefully adjust levels to ensure each instrument is audible. EQ is your best friend here. Use it to carve out space for each element, reducing frequencies that cause muddiness or harshness. For instance, use high-pass filters on guitars to clear up the low end for the bass and kick drum. Compression enhances clarity and control. Apply it to vocals and instruments to even out dynamics, but be cautious not to overdo it.

Adding reverb and delay helps recreate the live environment. Use reverb to simulate the space of the venue, applying it subtly to vocals and instruments to give them a sense of depth. Delay can be used creatively to add space and dimension. For instance, a short slapback delay on vocals can make them sit better in the mix. Editing and arranging the live tracks for a cohesive mix is the final step. Trim any unwanted noise or silence, and arrange the tracks to flow naturally. Crossfade between sections to ensure smooth transitions.

In the next chapter, we'll explore ways to enhance your learning experience, diving into interactive tools and online communities that can help you grow as an audio professional.

Chapter Fifteen

Enhancing Your Learning Experience

We remember the first time we listened to a professionally mixed track and noticed subtle details we had never paid attention to before—the crispness of the hi-hat, the smoothness of the vocal reverb, and the precise panning of the guitars. It was like discovering a whole new world hidden within the music. This revelation made us realize the importance of developing critical listening skills. Just as musicians practice their instruments, audio professionals must train their ears to become better at identifying and manipulating sound elements.

Using Interactive Tools to Train Your Ears

Ear training is a crucial aspect of audio production that often gets overlooked. Developing critical listening skills can significantly improve your ability to produce high-quality audio. It sharpens your ability to identify frequency ranges, recognize the effects of compression and EQ, and detect phase and timing issues. These skills are not innate; they can and should be developed and refined over time.

One of the most fundamental aspects of ear training is learning to identify different frequency ranges. This skill allows you to make precise EQ adjustments, ensuring each element in your mix has its own space and clarity. For instance, if you can pinpoint the muddiness in a vocal track, you can effectively cut the problematic frequencies, making the vocal sit better in the mix. Similarly, recognizing the presence of harsh high frequencies in a cymbal can help you tame it using a high-shelf EQ.

In addition to frequency identification, learning to recognize the effects of compression and EQ is vital. Compression can be subtle, making it challenging to hear its impact without trained ears. By practicing, you can learn to detect when a compressor is squashing the dynamics too much or when it's adding the perfect amount of punch to a drum track. EQ effects are equally important; understanding how boosting or cutting specific frequencies can shape a sound is essential for creating balanced mixes.

Phase and timing issues can wreak havoc on a mix if left unchecked. Being able to detect these problems quickly is crucial. For example, if two microphones are capturing the same sound source but are slightly out of phase, it can result in a thin and hollow sound. Recognizing and correcting these issues ensures your mixes remain full and cohesive.

Several ear training software and apps are available to help you hone these skills. Quiztones is a popular frequency training app with a simple interface and sleek design. It quizzes you on frequencies using samples from various instruments like drums, bass, guitar, and vocals. This app is excellent for identifying and matching frequencies, making it a valuable tool for any audio professional.

SoundGym offers a comprehensive ear training platform specifically tailored for audio engineers. It covers a wide range of topics, including frequency identification, EQ filter types, gain differences, and sound location/stereo impression. SoundGym provides daily workouts and quizzes that help you train your ears in a structured and engaging manner.

TrainYourEars EQ Edition focuses on EQ training, allowing you to learn how to make EQ corrections rather than guessing affected frequencies. This app enables you to design custom training programs, making it a flexible tool for addressing your specific needs.

Practical exercises using these interactive tools can significantly enhance your ear training. With Quiztones, you can start by identifying and matching frequencies. The app will play a tone, and you must select the correct frequency range. This exercise helps you become more familiar with different frequency ranges and their characteristics.

SoundGym offers daily ear training workouts that cover various aspects of audio production. By dedicating time each day to complete these workouts, you can gradually improve your critical listening skills. For example, you might practice identifying different EQ filter types or recognizing gain differences between two audio samples.

TrainYourEars provides exercises for practicing EQ adjustments. You can load an audio sample, apply an EQ change, and then try to match the original sound by making the opposite EQ adjustment. This exercise helps you understand how different frequencies interact and how EQ can shape a sound.

Integrating ear training into your daily practice is essential for continuous improvement. Set aside dedicated time each day for ear training, even if it's just 15 minutes. Consistency is key to developing and maintaining your skills. Using ear training apps during breaks or downtime can also be effective. For instance, you can complete a quick frequency identification quiz during a lunch break.

Tracking your progress and setting goals can keep you motivated. Many ear training apps allow you to monitor your performance over time. Use this feature to identify areas where you need improvement and set specific goals to address them. For example, you might aim to improve your accuracy in identifying frequencies by 10% over the next month.

Interactive Element: Ear Training Challenge

Try this exercise: Download Quiztones and start with the basic frequency identification quiz. Spend 10 minutes each day for a week practicing frequency identification. At the end of the week, note your improvement in accuracy. Next, move on to SoundGym and complete a daily workout for another week. Track your progress and compare your results from the start to the end of the week. Use TrainYourEars to practice EQ adjustments and see how accurately you can match the original sound after a week of daily practice.

Leveraging Online Communities for Feedback

Participating in online communities can be a game-changer for your audio production journey. Engaging with other audio professionals provides invaluable feedback and support, which can elevate the quality of your work. When you share your projects online, you receive constructive criticism that helps you see your work from different perspectives. This feedback can highlight areas you might have overlooked and offer fresh ideas for improvement. Additionally, you can learn from the experiences and insights of others, gaining knowledge about techniques, gear, and workflows that you might not have encountered on your own.

Building a network of like-minded individuals is another significant benefit of online communities. Connecting with other audio enthusiasts allows you to share your passion, exchange tips, and collaborate on projects. These connections can lead to lasting professional relationships and open doors to new opportunities. Whether you're seeking advice on a specific problem or looking for inspiration, online communities offer a wealth of resources and support.

Several popular online communities cater to audio professionals. Gearspace (formerly Gearslutz) is one of the largest audio engineering forums, offering discussions on a wide range of topics, including recording, mixing, mastering, and gear reviews. The forum is known for its knowledgeable user base and in-depth discussions, making it an excellent resource for both beginners and experienced professionals.

Reddit's r/audioengineering is an active subreddit dedicated to audio discussions. It's a great place to ask questions, share your work, and engage in conversations about various aspects of audio production. The community is friendly and supportive, making it an ideal platform for seeking advice and feedback.

Facebook groups like Audio Engineers and Home Recording Studio Zone are also valuable resources. These groups provide a platform for audio enthusiasts to share their projects, ask questions, and discuss gear and techniques. The communities are diverse, with members ranging from hobbyists to professionals, ensuring a broad spectrum of insights and experiences.

Discord servers such as Audio Production and Mixing & Mastering communities offer real-time interactions with other audio professionals. These servers have dedicated channels for different topics, including recording, mixing, mastering, and gear discussions. The real-time nature of Discord allows for immediate feedback and fosters a sense of community and collaboration.

It's important to participate effectively to get the most out of online interactions. When posting questions, provide detailed context to help others understand your situation and offer relevant advice. For example, if you're struggling with a mix, mention the specific elements you're having trouble with and describe your current setup and techniques. This information will enable others to give more accurate and helpful feedback.

Offering feedback and support to others is equally important. By sharing your insights and experiences, you contribute to the community's knowledge base and build goodwill. Engaging in discussions and providing constructive criticism can also reinforce your understanding of audio production concepts and techniques.

Following community guidelines and etiquette is crucial for maintaining a positive and productive environment. Respect others' opinions, avoid inflammatory language, and be open to different viewpoints. Remember that everyone is there to learn and grow, so fostering a supportive atmosphere benefits everyone involved.

Real-world examples highlight the benefits of active participation in online communities. For instance, an audio engineer once posted a mix on Gearspace seeking feedback. The community provided detailed suggestions on EQ adjustments, reverb settings, and overall balance. By incorporating this feedback, the engineer improved the mix significantly and gained new insights into mixing techniques.

Another example involves a collaborative project initiated through an online forum. A group of producers and engineers connected on Reddit's r/audioengineering and decided to work on a track together. Each member contributed their expertise, producing a polished final product showcasing their collective skills.

Testimonials from users of these online communities further emphasize their value. One user shared how the advice they received on a Facebook group helped them troubleshoot a persistent issue with their recording setup, saving them time and frustration. Another user mentioned how participating in Discord discussions broadened their understanding of different mixing approaches, enhancing their overall production quality.

Leveraging online communities for feedback and support is a powerful way to enhance your learning experience and improve your audio production skills. Engaging with other professionals, sharing your work, and contributing to discussions can provide valuable insights, foster connections, and open up new opportunities in the world of audio.

Accessing Additional Resources and Software

Staying updated with the latest resources and software is crucial for ongoing improvement in audio production. Continuously learning allows you to keep up with industry trends and advancements, expanding your knowledge and skill set. This constant growth provides access to new tools for creative exploration, ensuring your work remains fresh and innovative. The audio production landscape is ever-evolving, and adapting to these changes will keep you ahead of the curve, making your work relevant and competitive.

To further your understanding and expertise, several books, websites, and online courses offer valuable insights and practical knowledge. "Mixing Secrets for the Small Studio" by Mike Senior is an excellent resource that covers techniques for achieving professional-quality mixes in a home studio setting. Mike Senior's approachable writing style and practical advice make complex concepts easy to grasp. Another must-read is

"Mastering Audio" by Bob Katz, which delves into the intricacies of mastering, offering a deep understanding of the processes and techniques involved. This book is a staple in formal audio engineering education and is highly recommended for anyone looking to refine their mastering skills.

Websites like Sound on Sound and Pro Sound Web are treasure troves of information. Sound on Sound provides articles, reviews, and tutorials on various aspects of audio production, while Pro Sound Web offers forums and resources for professional audio engineers. Both platforms are excellent for staying updated with the latest industry news and trends. Additionally, online courses from LinkedIn Learning, Coursera, and Berklee Online offer structured learning paths that can help you build specific skills. These courses cover a wide range of topics, from the basics of audio production to advanced mixing and mastering techniques, providing a comprehensive educational experience.

In terms of software and plugins, several tools can significantly enhance your production process. Reaper and Studio One are two DAWs worth considering. Reaper is known for its flexibility and affordability, making it an excellent choice for those on a budget. It offers a customizable interface and a wide range of features, allowing you to tailor it to your workflow. Studio One, on the other hand, is praised for its fast workflow and intuitive design. It provides powerful tools for recording, mixing, and mastering, making it a favorite among many audio professionals.

When it comes to plugins, FabFilter Pro-Q is a go-to choice for EQ. Its intuitive interface and powerful features make it easy to shape your sound precisely. Waves SSL E-Channel is another excellent plugin, offering the classic sound of SSL consoles. It provides comprehensive channel strip functionalities, including EQ, compression, and gating, all modeled after the renowned SSL 4000 series. For virtual instruments, Native Instruments Komplete and Spectrasonics Omnisphere are top-notch options. Komplete offers a vast collection of instruments and effects, covering every aspect of music production. Omnisphere is known for its rich and diverse sound library, making it an invaluable tool for sound designers and music producers.

Evaluating and choosing the right resources and tools can be daunting, but a few strategies can help you make informed decisions. Reading reviews and testimonials from trusted sources can provide insights into the effectiveness and usability of a product. Websites like Sound on Sound and Gearspace often feature detailed reviews and user feedback, helping you understand the pros and cons of different options. Trying free trials and demos is another effective way to assess a tool's suitability for your needs. Many DAWs and plugins offer trial versions, allowing you to explore their features before making a purchase. This hands-on experience can give you a better sense of whether a tool fits your workflow and meets your expectations. Finally, consider your specific needs and goals when selecting resources. Think about the areas you want to improve or the skills you wish to develop, and choose tools and materials that align with those objectives. This targeted approach ensures that your investments in learning and equipment are purposeful and beneficial.

Resource List: Books, Websites, and Courses

Books:

- "Mixing Secrets for the Small Studio" by Mike Senior

- "Mastering Audio" by Bob Katz

Websites:

- Sound on Sound (www.soundonsound.com)

- Pro Sound Web (www.prosoundweb.com)

Online Courses:

- LinkedIn Learning (www.linkedin.com/learning)

- Coursera (www.coursera.org)

- Berklee Online (online.berklee.edu)

By continually accessing new resources and keeping your software updated, you can ensure that your skills and techniques remain sharp and relevant. The next chapter will delve into practical exercises and real-world projects to further enhance your audio production capabilities.

Chapter Sixteen

Interviews and Insights from Industry Experts

We remember the first time we met a renowned music producer. It was at a small industry event, and we were just another eager face in the crowd. But the words they shared about their journey, the struggles, and the triumphs left a lasting impact on me. It was inspiring to see how they made their mark in the music world and gave us hope that we could do the same. This chapter brings insights from some of the top music producers in the industry, offering a glimpse into their creative processes, career paths, and the ever-evolving landscape of music production.

Insights from Renowned Music Producers

One of the most insightful conversations we had was with Nascent, who is known for his work with SZA and Kanye West. Nascent started with Acid Pro and now uses Reason, favoring plug-ins like Keyscape for their ambient textures and nature sounds. He emphasized the importance of building leverage in the industry and being cautious of opportunities that seem too good to be true. Nascent's journey is a testament to the power of persistence and the importance of creating a unique sound. He often incorporates ambient textures and subtle nature sounds, pitched down to create a distinct atmosphere in his tracks.

Another enlightening interview was with Nova Wav, the duo behind hits for Beyoncé and Nicki Minaj. They started with FruityLoops and now use Pro Tools, known for their dark, melodic sound and strong songwriting. Nova Wav stressed the significance of staying true to one's musical roots while being open to exploring new genres. They are particularly interested in gospel music, despite being known for their hip-hop and R&B productions. Nova Wav's approach to collaboration and teamwork is notable; they believe in creating a comfortable studio environment where artists feel free to express their creativity.

Mike Hector, known for his work with Doja Cat and Kendrick Lamar, shared his unique approach to developing a sound. He avoids tutorials, preferring to experiment and find his own path. Mike's use of FL Studio and his desire to see a return to disco sounds highlight his innovative spirit. He believes over-reliance on Auto-Tune should be retired in favor of more authentic vocal performances. Mike's story is a powerful reminder of the importance of individuality in music production.

Jahaan Sweet, who has worked with Taylor Swift and Kendrick Lamar, provided valuable insights into the evolution of music production. Starting with GarageBand and now using Logic Pro X and FL Studio, Jahaan focuses on song clarity and making audio sound as clear as possible before mixing. He emphasized the transition from analog to digital production and how streaming services have revolutionized the industry. Jahaan's philosophy is that a song should be nearly perfect before it reaches the mixing stage, ensuring the final product is polished and professional.

Malibu Babie, known for her work with Nicki Minaj and Megan Thee Stallion, shared her journey from playing the piano to using Logic Pro X and Ableton 11. Her favorite plug-ins include Serum Synthesizer and Omnisphere. Malibu Babie incorporates unusual sounds like game alerts or water drops into her productions, creating a unique auditory experience. She expressed a desire to bring back the pop elements of 2008-2013 and retire the sad girl bedroom pop sound. Malibu Babie's innovative use of technology and her ability to blend different sounds are key to her success.

During these interviews, several common themes emerged. One is the importance of creativity in the studio. Whether it's incorporating ambient textures like Nascent or experimenting with unusual sounds like Malibu Babie, these producers emphasize the need to push boundaries and explore new possibilities. They also highlight the significance of collaboration. Nova Wav, for instance, creates a supportive and open environment for artists, allowing for the free flow of ideas.

Another crucial aspect is the evolution of music production. The transition from analog to digital has opened up new avenues for creativity. Jahaan Sweet discussed how digital audio workstations (DAWs) have democratized music production, making high-quality tools accessible to everyone. Streaming services have also changed the game, offering artists new ways to distribute music and connect with audiences.

One memorable anecdote came from Nascent, who recounted the challenge of producing a high-profile album under tight deadlines. Despite the pressure, he managed to create a standout track by incorporating ambient nature sounds, adding a unique touch that resonated with listeners. Another example is Nova Wav's innovative use of technology in a recent project, where they blended gospel elements with contemporary beats to create a fresh sound.

These insights from top producers underscore the importance of creativity, collaboration, and adaptability in the ever-changing world of music production. By learning from their experiences and applying their techniques, you can enhance your productions and carve out your unique space in the industry.

Interactive Element: Producer Techniques Journal Prompt

Reflect on a recent project and identify one area where you can incorporate a new technique inspired by these producers. Write down the steps you will take to implement this change and the expected outcome. This exercise will help you internalize and apply these insights to your work.

Tips from Leading Sound Designers

We had the chance to sit down with some of the industry's top sound designers. Their stories and insights were nothing short of inspiring. One of the most memorable conversations was with a sound designer who has worked on major films and video games. She started her career with a passion for music, which eventually led her to the world of sound design. Her journey took her through various projects, including indie films, blockbuster movies, and immersive video games.

She talked about her creative process, which often begins with understanding the narrative or the visual elements she's working with. She emphasized the importance of immersing oneself in the story to create sounds that truly enhance the experience. For a recent film, she spent days recording ambient sounds in different environments to capture the perfect background noise for a scene set in a bustling city. This attention to detail is what sets her work apart. She also shared that a portable recorder is one of her favorite tools, which allows her to capture unique sounds wherever she goes.

Another sound designer we spoke with has a background in theater and live performances. His approach to sound design is influenced by his experience working in different media. He explained that designing sound for theater requires a deep understanding of how sound interacts with physical space. This knowledge has been invaluable in his work on various projects, from live concerts to immersive theater experiences. He shared a story about designing sound for a critically acclaimed play, where he used a combination of live sound effects and pre-recorded audio to create an immersive environment for the audience.

Regarding practical advice, these sound designers had plenty to share. One of the key techniques they discussed is creating immersive soundscapes. This involves layering multiple sounds to create a rich and dynamic auditory experience. For example, in a scene set in a forest, you might layer the sound of rustling leaves, distant bird calls, and the gentle hum of insects. The goal is to create a soundscape that feels natural and enhances the visual elements without overpowering them.

Recording and manipulating sound effects is another crucial aspect of sound design. One designer shared his method for recording unique sounds, which often involves unconventional techniques. For a recent video game, he recorded the sound of breaking ice using various objects, from hammers to heavy boots. He then manipulated these recordings using software like Pro Tools and Ableton Live to create the desired effect. This process of experimentation and manipulation is key to creating sounds that stand out.

Integrating sound design with visual elements is another challenge that sound designers face. One designer explained that this requires close collaboration with the visual team to ensure the sound complements the visuals. For a film project, he worked closely with the director and the visual effects team to synchronize the sound of a spaceship landing with the visual effects. This involved multiple iterations and adjustments to get the timing and sound just right.

The challenges and rewards of sound design are numerous. Overcoming creative and technical challenges is a common theme. One sound designer shared a story about a project where he had to create the sound of a mythical creature. This involved a mix of animal sounds, synthesized effects, and human vocalizations. The technical challenge was to blend these elements seamlessly, which he achieved through meticulous editing and layering.

Balancing artistic vision with project requirements is another challenge. One designer talked about a project where the director had a very specific vision for the sound, which required a lot of back-and-forth to achieve. However, the satisfaction of creating impactful audio experiences makes all the challenges worthwhile. One designer recalled a memorable moment from a live sound design project, where the audience's reaction to a perfectly timed sound effect was incredibly rewarding.

These insights and stories from top sound designers highlight the creativity, dedication, and technical skills required in this field. By learning from their experiences and applying their techniques, you can enhance your sound design projects and create audio experiences that resonate with audiences.

Advice from Experienced Audio Engineers

Speaking with seasoned audio engineers offers a wealth of knowledge and practical insights that can elevate your audio production skills. One of the most memorable interviews was with Fitzville G. Martin, a blind audio engineer and CEO of Will Power Entertainment. His career path is both inspiring and educational. Fitzville started his journey in a small basement studio, driven by a passion for music and a keen ear. Despite the challenges, he built a successful business and produced award-winning music videos. Fitzville credits his mentors and early influences in shaping his technical approach and strong work ethic.

Fitzville's technical approach emphasizes meticulous planning and attention to detail. He shared his workflow for studio projects, which begins with a comprehensive pre-production phase. This includes detailed session planning, equipment checks, and setting up a signal flow chart. Fitzville believes that a well-organized session is the cornerstone of a successful recording. His experience spans various types of projects, from studio recordings to live broadcasts and even immersive audio for VR.

In a live broadcast setting, Fitzville faced a significant technical challenge. During a high-profile event, the main mixing console malfunctioned minutes before going live. With quick thinking and problem-solving skills, he rerouted the signal through backup equipment and managed to deliver a flawless broadcast. This experience underscores the importance of having a backup plan and being adaptable in high-pressure situations.

Another experienced audio engineer we spoke with, who has worked on studio and broadcast projects, shared valuable advice on achieving high-quality recordings. His approach involves using high-quality microphones and preamps, paying close attention to room acoustics, and ensuring proper gain staging. He emphasized the importance of capturing clean, unprocessed audio at the source, which provides more flexibility during mixing and mastering.

For mixing and mastering, he recommends starting with a well-balanced mix, focusing on achieving clarity and separation between elements. He uses a combination of EQ, compression, and reverb to shape the sound and create depth. One innovative technique he shared involves using parallel compression on drum tracks to add punch without sacrificing dynamics. This method involves creating a duplicate of the drum bus, applying heavy compression to the duplicate, and blending it with the original signal.

Troubleshooting and problem-solving are crucial skills for any audio engineer. One engineer recounted a session where a persistent hum in the recordings threatened to derail the project. After checking all cables and connections, he discovered a faulty power supply caused the issue. Replacing the power supply eliminated the hum, allowing the session to continue smoothly. This experience highlights the importance of systematically diagnosing issues and having spare equipment on hand.

The evolution of audio engineering has been remarkable. Advances in recording technology and equipment have significantly improved the quality and efficiency of audio production. The transition from analog to digital has revolutionized workflows, making editing, manipulating, and perfecting recordings easier. Digital audio workstations (DAWs) have become the central hub for audio production, offering powerful tools for recording, editing, and mixing. One engineer shared how the introduction of DAWs transformed his workflow, allowing for more creative freedom and precision.

Looking to the future, audio engineers are excited about emerging trends and innovations. Immersive audio technologies like Dolby Atmos and Auro-3D create new possibilities for three-dimensional soundscapes. AI and machine learning are automating tedious tasks, such as track categorization and initial mix balancing, freeing up engineers to focus on creative decisions. Cloud-based audio production enables real-time collaboration, making it easier for engineers to work remotely with clients and colleagues.

During one memorable session, an engineer recounted working with a renowned artist who wanted a unique vocal effect. After experimenting with various plugins and techniques, they achieved the desired sound by blending a distorted vocal track with a clean, reverb-heavy track. This innovative approach met the artist's vision and added a distinctive character to the recording.

The insights and experiences shared by these audio engineers offer valuable lessons in technical expertise, adaptability, and creativity. By applying their advice and learning from their experiences, you can confidently enhance your audio engineering skills and tackle any project.

As we wrap up this chapter, it's clear that the wisdom of experienced audio engineers can guide you through the complexities of audio production. Their stories and techniques emphasize the importance of preparation, creativity, and adaptability.

Conclusion

As we come to the end of "Mastering Audio Production at Home: The Complete Guide to Creating Professional Sound in Any Space," let's revisit our vision and purpose. This book aimed to empower you to achieve professional-quality audio production from the comfort of your home. Whether you're an audio engineer, music producer, sound designer, student, educator, content creator, musician, podcaster, or audio post-production professional, the goal has always been to make top-tier audio production accessible, practical, and budget-friendly.

Throughout this journey, we've covered a comprehensive array of topics. We began with the fundamentals of audio production, delving into signal flow and the basics of acoustics. From there, we explored setting up your home studio, providing detailed guidance on choosing the right space, implementing acoustic treatments, and selecting essential gear. We moved on to mastering your Digital Audio Workstation (DAW), ensuring you could confidently navigate software like Pro Tools, Ableton Live, and Logic Pro.

Recording techniques followed, where we discussed capturing vocals and acoustic instruments and using direct input for electric instruments. Achieving professional sound quality was next, focusing on noise reduction, effective EQ settings, and balancing levels. We then emphasized the importance of critical listening skills and creative sound design, showing you how to use effects, layering, and soundscapes to enhance your projects.

Mixing techniques were detailed, covering panning strategies, compression, and advanced reverb techniques. Mastering audio rounded out the technical sections, guiding you through preparing your mix for mastering and creating a master that translates across various playback systems. Troubleshooting common issues ensured you could tackle any challenges while staying current with industry trends and informed you about the latest tools and technologies.

Practical exercises and real-world projects offer hands-on experience, and insights from industry experts provide invaluable advice and inspiration. These elements combine to create a comprehensive and practical resource designed to help you achieve professional-quality audio production at home.

Key takeaways from this book include the importance of understanding signal flow and acoustics, the value of a well-organized home studio, and the power of mastering your DAW. Recording techniques and sound quality fundamentals are essential for capturing and refining your audio, while critical listening and creative sound design push your projects to the next level. Effective mixing and mastering ensure your final product sounds polished and professional, and staying current with industry trends keeps you ahead of the curve.

Now, it's time to take action. Apply what you've learned to your projects. Experiment with different techniques, and don't be afraid to make mistakes. Every misstep is an opportunity to learn and improve. Use the practical exercises and real-world projects as a starting point, and seek feedback from online communities and industry peers. Continuously refine your skills and stay updated with the latest tools and technologies.

Remember, the journey of mastering audio production is ongoing. There's always something new to learn, a new technique, or a new tool to explore. Embrace this journey with curiosity and passion. Your dedication and persistence will pay off, and the results will speak for themselves.

In closing, we want to leave you with this final encouragement: Believe in your ability to create professional-quality audio, regardless of your budget or experience level. The tools and knowledge are now at your fingertips. Your passion and creativity will drive you forward. Keep pushing boundaries, keep experimenting, and most importantly, keep creating. The world of audio production is vast and filled with endless possibilities. Your journey is just beginning, and we can't wait to see where it takes you.

References

- *Audio Signal Flow: What It Is and How to Use It* https://mastering.com/signal-flow/

- *DIY Acoustic Treatment for Your Home Studio: Step-by-* ... https://www.waves.com/diy-acoustic-treatment-home-studio-step-guide

- *The Audio Production Terms You Need To Know* https://www.spikeleo.com/blog/2020/8/26/the-audio-production-terms-you-need-to-know

- *Signal Problems & How To Avoid Them* https://www.soundonsound.com/techniques/signal-problems-how-avoid-them

- *The Ultimate Home Studio Setup Guide for 2024 on any* ... https://plus.pointblankmusicschool.com/the-ultimate-home-studio-setup-guide-for-2024-on-any-budget/

- *DIY Acoustic Treatment for Your Home Studio: Step-by-* ... https://www.waves.com/diy-acoustic-treatment-home-studio-step-guide

- *HOME STUDIO ESSENTIALS (for Beginners on a Budget)* https://audiouniversityonline.com/home-studio-essentials/

- *How to Soundproof a Home Studio for Recording - MasterClass* https://www.masterclass.com/articles/how-to-soundproof-a-home-studio

- *Pro Tools Basics 04: Interface Overview.* https://www.youtube.com/watch?v=AwJMSkdWDqA

- *Welcome to Live — Ableton Reference Manual Version 11* https://www.ableto n.com/en/manual/welcome-to-live/

- *Vocal Recording in Logic Pro X: A Comprehensive Guide ...* https://crate.fm/tu torials/vocal-recording-in-logic-pro-x-a-comprehensive-guide-for-beginners

- *Home Studio on a Budget: Getting Started for Less than ...* https://producelike apro.com/blog/home-studio-on-a-budget/

- *Best Portable Recording Booths That You Can Buy On- line* https://www.billboard.com/culture/product-recommendations/best-po rtable-recording-booths-buy-online-1235343112/

- *Mic Stuff: 7 Critical Tips on How to Mic an Acoustic Guitar* https://mxlmics.c om/7-critical-tips-on-how-to-mic-an-acoustic-guitar/

- *The DI Box - What Is It? Why Do I Need One? - InSync* https://www.sweetw ater.com/insync/di-boxes/

- *11 Common Vocal Production Mistakes in Home Studios* https://www.izotope.com/en/learn/11-common-vocal-production-mistakes-i n-home-studios.html?srsltid=AfmBOoqBs7alWXdZui0bHdW1W77G23Tm sVK629fzkKjcWHRVWvwh3I_i

- *Best Audio Noise Reduction Software* https://creativecow.net/forums/thread/ best-audio-noise-reduction-software/

- *Ultimate Guide: How to EQ Vocals for Begin- ners* https://www.izotope.com/en/learn/how-to-eq-vocals.html?srsltid=Afm BOooQfNEitUMrTQJu6PLpOUnM2owqDYXjcdKqli_s8o1a4l6rcWJm

- *Q. What's the difference between PPM and VU meters?* https://www.soundo nsound.com/sound-advice/q-whats-difference-between-ppm-and-vu-meters

- *How to Use Everything in iZotope Insight 2 | Intelligent ...* https://www.youtu be.com/watch?v=zBjdTQE3630

- *How to Develop Critical Listening Skills - Yamaha Music - Blog* https://hub.ya maha.com/audio/a-how-to/how-to-develop-critical-listening-skills/

- *Audio Frequencies Explained | Frequency Range Guide* https://mixingmonster.com/audio-frequencies/

- *10 Mixing Mistakes That are Easy to Fix* https://www.iconcollective.edu/mixing-mistakes

- *Ear Training for Audio Engineers – IMPROVE YOUR MIXES* https://audiouniversityonline.com/ear-training-for-mixing-engineers/

- *8 Creative Reverb Effects for Sound Design* https://www.izotope.com/en/learn/8-creative-reverb-effects-for-sound-design.html?srsltid=AfmBOorw7E5kl4WPwWRZkoC0t2Sujed_5FOHTVAYF_4eR-4ONDCQU9Vo

- *Layering Sounds: 20 Professional Strategies - Hyperbits* https://hyperbits.com/layering-sounds/#:~:text=Layering%20is%20when%20you%20combine,to%20create%20a%20textured%20downlifter.

- *Key Concepts in Sound Design for Film & Video Games* https://soundand.design/key-concepts-in-sound-design-for-film-video-games-227b96b890fd#:~:text=In%20film%2C%20sound%20is%20edited,dynamically%20to%20the%20game%20environment.

- *The Art of Foley: Creating Realistic Sound Effects in Post ...* https://c-istudios.com/the-art-of-foley-creating-realistic-sound-effects-in-post-production/#:~:text=of%20the%20film.-,Techniques%20used%20to%20create%20realistic%20Foley%20effects,are%20created%20using%20specific%20materials.

- *10 Tips for Better Mixes Through Panning* https://www.izotope.com/en/learn/10-tips-for-better-mixes-through-panning.html?srsltid=AfmBOor--Hq-g3OSoqdb8pabQUaGalq9hxei98OwGqxjZlYX5q8sCVSx

- *The best dynamic compression tips for beginners - Beat Spot* https://www.beatspot.pro/blogs/blog/the-best-dynamic-compression-tips-for-beginners

- *6 Creative Reverb Techniques in Music Production*

https://www.izotope.com/en/learn/6-creative-reverb-techniques-in-music-pro
duction.html?srsltid=AfmBOookbfZZ69-82FlQN7OiLtXBRV7U9mofChA
_feLdmWlyuieAxljF

- *Ultimate Guide to Panning Audio & Instruments in a Mix* https://www.avid
.com/resource-center/panning-audio-guide

- *Tips for Preparing a Mix for Mastering* https://www.abbeyroad.com/news/o
nline-mastering-abbey-roads-tips-for-preparing-a-mix-for-mastering-2559

- *6 Essential Mastering Tips For Music Producers* https://www.production-exp
ert.com/production-expert-1/6-essential-mastering-tips-for-music-producers

- *6 Tips for Creating Masters that Translate Well to All Systems* https://www.sonarworks.com/blog/learn/6-tips-for-creating-masters-th
at-translate-well-to-all-systems

- *What Is Metering in Mixing and Mastering? - iZotope*
https://www.izotope.com/en/learn/what-is-metering-in-mixing-and-masterin
g.html#:~:text=In%20mixing%20and%20mastering%2C%20metering,stereo%
20spread%2C%20and%20dynamic%20range.

- *How to Fix Distorted Audio: Complete Guide - Boris FX*
https://borisfx.com/blog/how-to-fix-distorted-audio/#:~:text=The%20proble
m%20may%20be%20from,equipment%20can%20cause%20distorted%20audi
o.

- *How to Fix Audio Clipping: 8 Tips and Methods* https://borisfx.com/blog/ho
w-to-fix-audio-clipping-8-tips-and-methods/

- *Synchronization problems and solutions in Logic Pro for
Mac* https://support.apple.com/guide/logicpro/synchronization-problems-a
nd-solutions-lgcpfffba0c7/mac

- *Phase Alignment Plugins: Perfect Your Mix!* https://solarheavystudios.com/p
hase-alignment-plugins-perfect-your-mix/

- *10 AI Tools For Music Producers That Are Actually Useful*

https://theproducerschool.com/blogs/featured-blogs/10-ai-tools-for-music-pr
oducers-that-are-actually-useful?srsltid=AfmBOoqROCSohaytUJhiLkxvY_I
bkh9NGnQ27OyiUPnSWVH7aDV1-CPO

- *Binaural Recording Techniques - The Complete Guide* https://www.dpamicro
phones.com/mic-university/binaural-recording-techniques

- *The Future of Music Rights Management with
Blockchain* https://medium.com/@rittik.rtk/the-future-of-music-rights-man
agement-with-blockchain-a-simple-guide-34d6b807f49c

- *BandLab | FREE Online DAW Award-Winning Features* https://www.band
lab.com/creation-features?lang=en

- *The 5 best budget audio interfaces for $200, $100, and $50* https://higherhz.co
m/best-budget-audio-interfaces/

- *DIY Acoustic Panels : 11 Steps (with Pictures)* https://www.instructables.com/
DIY-Acoustic-Panels-1/

- *Focusrite Scarlett 4th Gen* https://www.soundonsound.com/reviews/focusrite
-scarlett-4th-gen

- *14 Best Free DAWs for 2024 (July 2024 Update)* https://blog.landr.com/best
-free-daw/

- *The Importance of Taking Notes on a Recording Session* https://theproaudiofil
es.com/the-power-of-taking-notes-on-a-session/

- *The Importance of Taking Notes on a Recording Session* https://theproaudiofil
es.com/the-power-of-taking-notes-on-a-session/

- *A guide to technical report writing* https://www.theiet.org/media/5182/techn
ical-report-writing.pdf

- *Audio-Visual Format Documentation Project: Background
... * https://www.digitizationguidelines.gov/guidelines/FADGI-AV_AppSpec
Proj_Bkgd_101007.pdf

- *Which Are the Best Free DAWs for Music Production in 2023?* https://info.xp osuremusic.com/article/best-free-daw

- *How to Mix Music: A Complete Guide to Audio Mixing* https://www.avid.co m/resource-center/how-to-mix-music

- *Film Sound Design | Laetro* https://www.laetro.com/blog/film-sound-design-crafting-emotion-through-s oundsc#:~:text=By%20carefully%20choosing%20and%20layering,the%20worl d%20of%20the%20film.

- *How to Record a Live Music Session - What Do I Need?* https://arcussounds.com/what-do-i-need-recording-live-music-guide/#:~:text =Pro%20Tips%20for%20Recording%20Live%20Music%20Successfully&text =Choose%20WAV%20Format%3A%20The%20WAV,you%20find%20your%2 0perfect%20setup.

- *Ear Training Apps: The 8 Best Tools For Improving Your ...* https://blog.landr. com/best-ear-training-apps/

- *The Top 5 Best Music Production Forums* https://www.blackghostaudio.com/ blog/the-top-5-best-music-production-forums

- *The 11 Best Music Production Books You Need to Read in ...* https://blog.landr .com/music-production-books/

- *The Best Digital Audio Workstations (DAWs) for 2024* https://www.pcmag.c om/picks/the-best-audio-editing-software

- *How Five Top Producers Are Making Music in 2023* https://www.billboard.com/music/rb-hip-hop/producers-2023-intervie w-nascent-nova-wav-1235193591/

- *The Evolution of Music Production Technologies* https://thecomposerclass.com/articles/the-evolution-of-music-production-tec hnologies-a-deep-dive-into-the-history-and-development-of-music-production -technologies-from-analog-to-digital

- *The Future of Audio Engineering: Trends and Innovations* https://www.mi.edu/in-the-know/future-audio-engineering-trends-innovations-industry/

- *Career Conversations: Interview with a Blind Audio Engineer* https://www.youtube.com/watch?v=DTQ3YL0LZGo